Eleazar Albin

Natural History of English Song-Birds

Eleazar Albin

Natural History of English Song-Birds

ISBN/EAN: 9783337181321

Printed in Europe, USA, Canada, Australia, Japan

Cover: Foto ©ninafisch / pixelio.de

More available books at **www.hansebooks.com**

Frontispiece

Publish'd June 12, 1779, by T. Lowndes N.º 77 Fleet Street.

A NATURAL HISTORY

OF

ENGLISH SONG-BIRDS,

INCLUDING SUCH

FOREIGN BIRDS

AS ARE USUALLY BROUGHT OVER AND ESTEEMED
FOR THEIR SINGING:

Their proper Management, Diseases, and Cures.

TO WHICH ARE ADDED,

FIGURES OF THE COCK, HEN, AND EGG OF EACH SPECIES,

EXACTLY COPIED FROM NATURE,

By Mr. ELEAZAR ALBIN,

AND CURIOUSLY ENGRAVEN ON COPPER.

A NEW EDITION CORRECTED,

WITH SEVERAL IMPROVEMENTS, UNDER THE ARTICLE OF

CANARY-BIRDS.

LONDON:

Printed for T. LOWNDES, Nº 77, in *Fleet-Street*, and S. BLADON, in *Paternoster-Row*. 1779.

Price 3s. plain, and 7s. 6d. coloured.

TO THE
READER.

SINGING-BIRDS are so pleasant a part of the Creation; whether we consider their variety, beauty, or harmony; that the animal world does not afford more agreeable objects to the eyes, nor that so sweetly gratifies the sense of hearing: they were, undoubtedly, designed by the great Author of Nature to entertain and delight mankind, who, for the generality, are well pleased with these pretty innocent creatures. I therefore thought I could not do a more acceptable service for the lovers of these sweet choristers of the woods, considering that it had never been yet done with such useful improvements, than to furnish them with instructions for preserving them in their houses, because they cannot always be entertained with their musick in the fields.

TO THE READER.

To which end, in a concife, methodical manner, I have given the defcription, character, &c. of each fpecies; the marks of cock and hen; the time and manner of building their nefts; the number, colour, &c. of their eggs; how to order and bring up the young; and whatever elfe is neceffary to be known for breeding them. And, to render it ftill more ufeful and entertaining, there are added the reprefentations of the cock, hen, and egg of each fort, exactly copied from nature. This laft very pleafant, and fuitable addition, which is univerfally delightful to all perfons, is wanting in the books that have been hitherto publifhed on this fubject.

I fhall obferve nothing more, only, that I wifh my readers may receive the fatisfaction that was intended, by the fincere endeavours of their

Moft humble fervant,

A Bird Fancier.

Black-Bird, Cock, Hen & Egg

A
NATURAL HISTORY
OF
ENGLISH SINGING-BIRDS.

The Description and Character of the Black-Bird.

THIS is a well-known bird, being common in most, if not all the counties in England; therefore needs not a particular description. He is the largest songbird that I know of, found in this kingdom; and likewise one of the first that proclaims the welcome spring, by his shrill harmonious voice, as if he were the harbinger of nature, to awaken the rest of the feathered tribe to prepare for the approaching season: and by the sweet modulation of his tuneful accents,

accents, endeavours to delight the hen, and allure her to submit to his embraces, even before there are leaves on the trees, and whilst the frosts are in the fields; building their nest the soonest of any bird; having young ones, commonly by the twenty-fifth of March, and sometimes by the middle of that month.

The cock, when kept in a cage, whistles and sings very delightfully all the spring and summer-time; at least four or five months in the year: is a stout, hardy bird; which, besides his own pleasant natural note, may be taught to whistle, or play a tune.

The Black-bird, when wild in the fields, feeds promiscuously upon berries and insects; 'tis a solitary bird, that for the most part flies singly.

The distinguishing Marks of the Cock and Hen.

THEY are not easily known by their colour while young, but the blackest bird generally proves a cock: the irides, or circle, that circumvests the eye in the young cock-bird, is yellow: his bill is black, and turns not perfectly yellow till he is near a year old: the bill of an old cock-bird is of a deep yellow; in the hen the tip and upper part is black; the mouth, in both,

is

is yellow within: the hen, and young cock-birds are rather brown, or of a dark ruffet, than black, and their bellies of an afh-colour; but after the cock has mewed his chicken feathers, he becomes coal-black.

The Time and Manner of the Black-bird's *building her Neſt, &c.*

THIS bird, as I obſerved before, breeds very ſoon in the year; has young ones by the end of *March*, or ſooner: ſhe builds her neſt very artificially; the outſide of moſs, ſlender twigs, bents and fibres of roots, all very ſtrongly cemented, and joined together with clay; plaiſtering the inſide alſo, and lining it with a covering of ſmall ſtraws, bents, hair, or other ſoft matter; upon which ſhe lays four or five eggs, ſeldom more, of a blueiſh green colour, full of duſky ſpots. She builds pretty open, generally in a hedge, near the ground, and before there are many leaves upon the buſhes; which ſo expoſes their neſt, conſidering the largeneſs of it, that it may be eaſily diſcovered.

The cavity of a complete neſt I meaſured, was two inches and an half deep; diameter at the top, four inches one way, and five the other, being of an oblong figure: it weighed thirteen ounces: the bird itself is in length, from the tip of the bill to the end of the tail, eleven inches, of which the bill is one inch, and the tail four inches long.

Of the young Birds, and how to order them.

THE Black-bird has either four or five young ones at a breeding, hardly ever more or less; you may take them at twelve days old, or sooner; they may be raised with little trouble, taking care to keep them clean, and feeding them with sheep's heart, or other lean meat, that is not salted, cut very small, and mixed with a little bread; and while young, give them their meat moist, and feed them every two hours, or thereabouts; when they are grown up, feed them with any sort of flesh meat, raw or dressed, provided it be not salt; it will be rather better food for them, if you mix a little bread with it. When their nest grows foul, take them out, and put them into a cage or basket, upon clean straw; and when they can feed themselves, separate them.

He is a stout healthful bird, not very subject to disorders; but, if you find him sick or droop at any time, an house spider or two

two will help him; and let him have a little cochineal in his water, which is very chearful and good. They love to wash and prune their feathers; therefore, when they are fully grown up, set water in their cages for that purpose.

It is to be remembered as a general rule, to give all your birds wholesome good food, never letting it grow stale or sour; and to be ever mindful of keeping their cages clean: these are the surest means to make all kinds of birds thrive, and to prevent many diseases they are subject to from nastiness and unwholesome food and water.

Black-birds are always brought up from the nest, the old ones not being to be tamed.

Of the Song-thrush.

The Description and Character.

THE common Song-thrush is somewhat less than the Black-bird: the upper surface of the body is of an olive colour, with a mixture of yellow in the wings; the breast yellowish, spotted with dusky spots, and the belly white.

There are three or four other sorts of Thrushes found in England; as first, the great Thrush, called the Missel-bird, Measle-taw, or Shrite, which in the colour and spots of the breast and belly, agrees with the Song-thrush, but is a bigger bird: he is very beautiful to look at, but not valued for singing, therefore seldom kept in a cage.

The second sort, called the Redwing, Swinepipe, or Wind-thrush, is in shape and colour so like the Song-thrush, that they are hard to be distinguished, only the latter hath more, and greater spots on the breast and belly, and is somewhat bigger: this kind is in no esteem for singing. It is a bird of passage, that shifts places according to the seasons of the year; but whither it goes, is not to us perfectly known.

Song Thrush, Cock, Hen & Egg.

The third sort is called the small Heath-thrush, from its building upon heaths and commons; he is of a darker colour than any of the other of the Thrush kind, and by some valued for singing; but as none of the sorts are comparable to the common Song-thrush, nor so well known, I shall treat of the Song-thrush only; which is a curious bird, as well for the great variety of his notes, as his long continuance in song, which is, at least, nine months in the year. In the beginning of the spring, he sits on high trees, and sings most sweetly, and is as delightful a bird as a person can desire to keep in a cage; some of them, when they have been brought up from the nest, have learnt the Wood-lark's, Nightingale's, and other curious birds songs.

The distinguishing Marks of the Cock and Hen.

THE cock and hen of this kind are so much alike in the colour of their feathers, and shape of their bodies, that, notwithstanding I have carefully examined them divers times, I could not discover any certain marks, whereby to know the one from the other: yet, thus much I have discovered, which will appear to a nice observer:—in a full-feathered bird, the dusky, or olive

colour

colour on his back, &c. is somewhat darker than the back, &c. of the hen-bird; and has a more glossy cast; the spots on his breast and belly seem darker, and brighter likewise, and rather more white appears on his belly.

It is observable, that in the cocks and hens of all kinds of birds, where the colours are the same in both, yet the cock-bird constantly excels the hen in the resplendency of his feathers: in the Song-thrush, in an old bird, this difference is apparent; but then we are not put to such difficulties to know the cock, he sufficiently discovers himself by his fine song.

In young Thrushes, I would always chuse the sleekest and brightest bird; when they begin to feed themselves, both cocks and hens will record: the cock will get upon his perch, and sing his notes low, for some time; the hen will attempt to sing, but do it only by jerks, and so disappoint your expectation. At the latter end of the summer, when their moulting is over, the cocks will break out strong in song, and sing in winter, as well as summer.

The Time and Manner of the building her Nest.

THIS bird breeds very early in the spring, nearly as soon as the Black-bird;
she

she commonly has young ones by the end of March, or beginning of April. I saw a neſt of young, about the fifth or ſixth of April, notwithſtanding it had been a cold ſpring, which were well feathered, and at leaſt twelve days old.

The Thruſh builds in woods or orchards, ſometimes in a thick hedge, near the ground. The outſide of her neſt conſiſts of fine ſoft green moſs, interwoven with dead graſs, hay, &c. The inſide very curiouſly plaiſtered with cow-dung, not daubed, as ſome have ſaid, but with better ſkill than many of our plaiſterers could do the ſame work. Note, the Black-bird always plaiſters with clay or mud, this bird always with cow-dung; the other lays a covering of ſoft ſtuff in the inſide to lay her eggs upon; the Thruſh lays her's upon the bare inſide or plaiſtering, but not till it is thoroughly dry; five or ſix in number, of a blueiſh green colour, ſpeckled with a few ſmall black ſpots, chiefly at the biggeſt end.

The hollow of a compleat neſt I meaſured, was two inches and a half deep; the diameter of the inſide at the top four inches; it was exactly round, and the whole neſt weighed one ounce and three quarters.—I examined two more at the ſame time, which were nearly of the ſame dimenſions with this, but in weight, one three ounces, the

other

other three and an half. The length of a full-grown bird, from the point of the bill to the end of the tail, is nine inches; of which the bill is one, and the tail three and a half; therefore, allowing for tail, bill, and head, which always lie out when she sits in her nest, the cavity is just fitted to receive her body. The same I have observed of the nests of some other birds; especially such as build with sides, and make deep cavities. The bird stands within side, when she is at work, and makes her own body the model of her dimensions, in building.

Of the Young, *how to order them, &c.*

THE Song-thrush has five or six young ones at a breeding; they may be taken at twelve or fourteen days old, or sooner if it be mild weather; they must be kept warm and clean, and fed with raw meat, bread, and hemp-seed bruised; the meat cut small, and the bread a little wet, and then mixed together: feed them once in about two hours. You must be sure to keep them very neat and clean; take their dung away every time you feed them: when their nest grows very foul, take them out, and put them in clean straw; and when they are pretty well feathered, put them in a large cage with two or three perches in it, and dry mofs or ftraw at the bottom. When they are grown up, you may feed them with flefh meat, boiled, raw, or roafted, provided it be not falt; or you may by degrees intirely wean them of flefh, and give them only bread and hemp-feed; but I approve of flefh, mixed with bread, as the beft food. Give them frefh water twice a week to wafh themfelves; otherwife they will not thrive: if they are kept dirty, it will give them the cramp, to which they are very fubject. Good victuals, water, and clean lodging, are the beft means to prevent it.

The Thrufh, when in the fields, feeds on infects and fnails, as alfo berries of white thorn and mifletoe.

Of the Starling.

The Description and Character.

THE Starling is nearly as big as the Black-bird, and in shape very much like that bird. It does not sing naturally, but has a wild, screaming, uncouth note; yet for his aptness in imitating man's voice, and speaking articulately, and his learning to whistle divers tunes, is highly valued as a very pleasant bird; and when well taught, will sell for five guineas or more.

They are gregarious birds, living and flying together in great flocks: they company also with Redwings and Fieldfares; yet they do not fly away with them, but abide with us all the year.

The Marks of the Cock and Hen.

THERE is a mark peculiar to the cock of this kind, whereby he may be known from the hen, whilst young. Under his tongue he has a black stroke, very plain to be seen if you open his mouth, which the hen hath not, or, at least, so faint, that 'tis hardly visible; but the first time the

cock

Starling, Cock, Hen, and Egg.

cock moults his feathers, he loses that black stroke: he may then be known from the hen by his colours, in the beauty of which he much excels her. His breast has a changeable cast of green, red, purple, &c. else the feathers all over his body are black, with a blue and purple gloss, varying, as it is variously exposed to the light; only the tips of the feathers on his head, neck, and breast are yellowish; and on the belly, &c. white: all his spots and colours are brighter than those of the hen. The bill of the cock is of a pale yellow, inclining to white; in the hen, dusky.

The Time and Manner of the Starling's *building her nest.*

THIS bird usually breeds in May, has young ones fit to take towards the end of that month, sometimes by the middle of it. They build their nest in the holes of towers, pigeon-houses, trees, &c. The goodness of these birds does not depend upon the places where they breed, though some have given the preference to one sort, and some to the other; for my part, I could never find such a difference as to esteem one sort before the other, for the same birds may build in any of those places, as they find it

most

most convenient for them. She lays four or five eggs, lightly tinctured with a greenish blue.

Of the Young, how to order them, &c.

THE Starling has four or five young ones at a breeding; they may be taken when double pen-feathered, which is about ten days old; taking the same care in keeping them very clean and warm, as was directed in the Black-bird and Thrush: you may put them in a basket in clean straw, and bring them up with the same meat, and after the same manner as young Black-birds, feeding them every two hours, five or six small pieces at a time; let them have enough, but never overload the stomachs of young birds, it does them more harm than good. Every time you feed, or take them in hand, you may talk to them what you would have them learn; they are apt birds, and will take it presently. To slit their tongues, as many people advise and practise, that the birds, as they say, may talk the plainer, is a cruel and useless expedient; they will talk as well without, as I have found by experience; as will likewise Magpies, and other talking birds. When they can feed themselves, put them in a large [*you may bring them up to Wood larks*] meat large cage, with clean ſtraw or moſs at the bottom, and give them ſometimes clean water to waſh themſelves in; this is the moſt ſure method to have good healthful birds, ſuch as will reward your trouble in bringing them up. The Starling, when wild, feeds upon beetles, worms, and other inſects.

The length of a full-grown bird, from the tip of his bill to the end of his tail, is nine inches; of which the bill is an inch and a quarter, and the tail three inches long; and, when in fleſh, weighs about three ounces.

The bird is naturally hardy and healthful; but when kept in a cage, is ſubject to the cramp, fits, &c. ſometimes it ſeizes him ſo ſuddenly, that he will fall down from his perch, and beat himſelf to death preſently; a ſpider, or meal-worm is a good remedy againſt it, giving him two or three at a time, twice or thrice a week. If you give him good meat and drink, as I ſaid by the Black-bird, and keep him clean, it will prevent his fits, or any other diſorder, better than any thing elſe that I know of.

Of the Bullfinch.

The Description and Character.

BULLFINCHES are so called from their heads, which are black, and, for the proportion of their bodies, large: in some places in England, they are called Nopes, in others, Thick-bills, and in some Hoops: this last name they have, probably, from their wild hooping sort of a note. They are very docile birds, the hen learning after the pipe or whistle, as well as the cock, having no song of their own, but what is taught them, in which they excel most birds: and the peculiar rarity of these birds is, that they never forget what they have once learnt, though they hang among ever so many birds. Some have been taught to speak several words at command. 'Tis a bird much esteemed in England, both for beauty and singing; and deservedly, in my judgment; for, in the former, he equals, and the latter, when well taught, excels all small birds: they have been frequently sold from five to ten guineas a bird.

These birds delight to feed upon the buds of fruit-trees, such as the apple, pear, peach, and other garden trees; of which they only take the blowing buds, and by that means

P. 16.

do great damage to the gardeners; who, therefore, hate and destroy them, as a great pest of their gardens. They say, in some part of the kingdom, a reward is given by the churchwardens for every Bullfinch that's killed; if so, that may be assigned as one reason of their scarcity; being less common than most other singing-birds that breed with us.

The Marks of the Cock and Hen.

THE cock is in bigness equal to the hen, but hath a flatter crown, and excels her in beauty of his colours; a lovely scarlet, or crimson, adorns his breast; the feathers on the crown of the head, and those that compass the bill, are of brighter black than those of the hen: if both are seen together, the one may very easily be known from the other; the colours in the cock being much more resplendent than in the hen: but whilst the birds are young, it is more difficult to distinguish them: one of the surest ways is, to pull off a few feathers from their breasts when they are about three weeks old, and in about ten or twelve days after, you will perceive the feathers to come where you have pulled, of a curious red, if a cock; if a hen, they will come of a palish brown.

The Time, Manner, &c. of her building.

THE Bullfinch breeds late in the spring; seldom has young ones before the end of May, or beginning of June: she builds in an orchard, wood, or park, where there are plenty of trees, or on heaths: her nest is not very common to be found; 'tis an ordinary mean fabric, made with seemingly little art: she lays four or five eggs, of a blueish colour, spotted at the biggest end with large dark brown, and faint reddish spots.

Of the Young, how to order them, &c.

YOU must not take these birds too young; let them be well feathered first, at least twelve or fourteen days old; keep them warm and clean, feed them every two hours, from morning until night, giving them little at a time: their meat must be rape-feed soaked in clean water, eight or ten hours; then scalded, strained, and bruised, mixt with an equal quantity of white bread soaked in fair water, boiled with a little milk to a thick consistency: make but little at a time, but let them have fresh every day, it being apt to sour in two days, and such meat will spoil the birds: when they begin to feed themselves; break them from this

soft

ENGLISH SINGING-BIRDS.

foft meat as foon as you can; then give them rape and canary feed, the fame as you do the Linnet, but more of the former than the latter. If at any time you perceive them out of order, put a blade of faffron in their water; and you may try them with the Wood-lark's meat, or fine hemp-feed, but keep moftly to rape, with a little canary-feed mixed with it.

You muft remember often to pipe, whiftle, or talk to them, whilft they are young, what you are minded they fhould learn, and you will find them foon take it.

A Bullfinch, at full growth, is fix inches long, from point of bill to the end of the tail, of which the tail is two inches: in weight thirteen drams.

The Bullfinch, in its wild state, has only a plain note; but when tamed becomes remarkably docile, and may be taught any tune after a pipe, or to whistle any notes in the finest manner: it seldom forgets what it has learnt. It will become so tame as to come at call, perch on its masters shoulder and (at command) will go through a difficult musical lesson.

Of the Goldfinch,

Which in some Places, from its feeding on the Seeds of Thistles, is called Thistlefinch.

The Description and Character.

IT is every where in England well-known, and highly esteemed both for singing and for the elegancy of its colours, being certainly the most beautiful and finest-feathered of all cage-birds: a ring of curious scarlet-coloured feathers encompasses the fore-part of his head, or basis of the bill; and from the eyes to the bill on each side, is drawn a black line; the jaws are white, the top of the head black, from which a broad black line is produced on both sides, almost to the neck; the hinder part of the head is white; the neck and fore-part of the back are of a reddish ash-colour; the rump, breast, and sides of the same, but a little paler; the belly whitish; the wings and tail black, only the tips of the principal feathers in both are white; besides, the wings are adorned with a most beautiful transverse stroke of yellow or gold-colour. I should not have been so particular in describing the colours of this bird, but I think the great

variety

Goldfinch, Cock, Hen, and Egg.

variety that Nature has painted it with, wherein it excels all small birds, at least what are found in these parts of the world, make it deserving of it; yet, by reason of age, sex, or other accidents, the Goldfinch sometimes varies from these colours.

They are of a mild and gentle nature, as may even thence appear, that presently after they are caught, without using any art or care, they will fall to their meat and drink; nor are they so affrighted at the presence of a man as most other birds are wont to be, nor very much troubled at their imprisonment in a cage; for, if they have continued there a good while, they like it so well, that though you let them loose, they will not fly away; but when scared, fly directly to their cage for shelter.

They are called in some places, Draw-waters, from their aptness to learn to draw their water when they want to drink, in a little ivory bucket, fastened to a small chain, made for that purpose: 'tis a pretty sight to see with what dexterity these little creatures will pull up their bucket, drink, and throw it down again; and lift up the lid of a small box, or bin, with their bill, to come at their meat, &c. They are wonderfully delighted with viewing themselves in a glass, fixed to the back of their bucket-board, where they will sit upon their perch, pruning and dres-

sing

sing themselves with the greatest care imaginable, often looking in the glass, and placing every feather in the nicest order; no lady can take greater pleasure, or be more nice in dressing herself, than this little beautiful bird is in rectifying all disorders in his plume, not suffering a feather to lay amiss.

The Goldfinch is a long-lived bird, that will sometimes reach to the age of twenty years: Mr. Willoughby makes mention of one that lived twenty-three years. They are birds that fly in flocks, or companies; and when at liberty, delight to feed upon the seeds of thistle, teasel, hemp, dock, &c.

The Marks of the Cock and Hen.

THE feathers on the ridge of the wing in the cock are coal-black, quite up to the shoulder, whereas in the hen-bird, though they appear black, are of a grey, or dusky ash-colour, when compared to those of the cock: he is browner on the back and sides of the breast; the red, yellow, and, in short, all his colours are much brighter than those of the hen: these are constant, infallible marks, by which the cock may be known from the hen, either old or young: besides, the hen hath a smaller note, and sings not so much.

The Time, Manner, &c. of building their Nest.

THE Goldfinch begins to build in April, when the fruit-trees are in blossom: as they excel all our small birds in beauty of feathers, so do they likewise in art: their nest is not only very small, but exceeding pretty; the outside consists of very fine moss, curiously interwoven with other soft bedding; the inside lined with delicate fine down, wool, &c. She lays six or seven white eggs, specked and marked with a reddish brown. To find their nest is not very easy, for they generally build in fruit-trees, viz. apple, pear, plumb, &c. but most commonly in the apple, pretty high upon the branches, where either the blossom or leaves intercept our sight; and at such a time when we cannot come at them without the hazard of damaging the bloom, or young fruit. I have known these birds very often to build in the elder-tree; and sometimes in thorns and hedges; but not near so common as in fruit-trees.

Of the Young, how to order them, &c.

THE Goldfinch has six or seven young ones at a breeding; they are tender birds, and therefore should not be taken too soon; let them be pretty well feathered first; they will not be sullen, like the young of many other birds, by staying too long in the nest; when you take them, prepare their meat after this manner:—soak white bread in fair water, strain it, and then boil it with a little milk, till 'tis as thick as hasty-pudding, adding to it a little flour of canary-seed; with this meat feed them every two hours, or oftner, giving them but little at a time, two or three small bits only; begin to feed them about sun-rising, and continue after this manner till sun-setting: let them have fresh victuals every day, or every other day at farthest; when you have fed them a month, or thereabouts, begin to break them from this soft meat, by giving them a little canary-seed, and soft meat besides; when you find they feed pretty freely upon the seed, keep them constantly to that diet; but though they will eat hemp-seed, and some other kinds of seed, yet I never found it agree so well with them as the canary.

If a young Goldfinch be brought up under the Canary-bird, the Wood-lark, or any other fine-singing bird, he will take their song very readily: I am told of a lady that has one of these birds, that will talk very finely.

A cock-bird, bred from the nest, will couple with a hen Canary-bird, and produce
a bird

a bird between both kinds; partaking of the fong and colours of both.

The length of a full-grown bird, from the tip of his bill to the end of his tail, is five inches and a half; of which the latter is two, and the former a little more than half an inch long; when in flefh the bird weighs about an ounce.

This, as I faid before, is a long-lived and very healthful bird, that is feldom out of order; but when I find him droop, I give him faffron in his water; if he has a fcouring, crumble a little dry chalk in his cage, or among his feed, or ftick a bit betwixt the wires of his cage, and gravel at the bottom, and try him with a little thiftle-feed, or other feeds which they delight to feed upon when wild: the firft may be found in the great thiftle, at the bottom of a white down.

Thefe birds are taken almoft at any time of the year, either with lime-twigs, or the clap-net, in great numbers; the young flight in June, July, or Auguft; but the beft time for catching them is about Michaelmas: they frequent the fields where the thiftle, and thofe other feeds grow, as mentioned before: they are eafily caught, being of fo gentle and familiar a nature, and will both feed and fing prefently; when

when you firſt take them, you may give them hemp-ſeed cracked, or ſome of the ſame they love to feed upon in the fields; you may ſoon bring them to feed on the canary, which is more wholeſome, and agrees better with them than hemp-ſeed.

Chaffinch, Cock, Hen, and Egg.

Of the Chaffinch.

The Description and Character.

THE Chaffinch is a stout, hardy, well-known bird; being common almost in every tree or hedge; of the bigness of the Bullfinch; lavish in his song, and when brought up from the nest, or branchers, will sing six or seven months in the year; the wild, not above three months; and chiefly in breeding-time. Some of these birds prove good and valuable, but the greater part not worth keeping.

'Tis a custom among the bird-men, when they want to learn the Chaffinch a song, to blind him when he is about three or four months old; which is done by closing up his eyes with a wire made almost red-hot, because, as they say, he will be more attentive, and learn the better; but I am sure it would be much better never to confine them in cages, than purchase their harmony by such diabolical usage. It is enough, to deprive these little innocent creatures of liberty for our pleasure and entertainment; but to put out their eyes to encrease it, is exceedingly barbarous. If what they assign for this, is true, yet the practice is cruel, and

and what no one, who has any tenderneſs in his nature, would ever be guilty of. This poor bird, beſides the pain of the firſt operation, and what he ſuffers before, to prepare him for it, by being kept in darkneſs till he can find his meat, &c. and the miſery that follows for a fortnight, or more, is ſometimes tortured a ſecond time, becauſe, perhaps, he has rubbed his eyes open again, or the cruelty was too favourably performed.

The Marks of the Cock and Hen.

THE male of this kind may be diſtinguiſhed from the female, at ten or twelve days old; the difference is very plain, if you view them together: the cock-bird has a great deal more white in his wing than the hen, particularly on his pinion; his breaſt is remarkably redder, and the feathers of the whole bird of a higher and brighter colour than the hen's. In an old bird, the head of the cock is blueiſh, the back of a reddiſh brown, with a mixture of aſh-colour or green; the breaſt of a fine red; and the belly, under the tail, white. The colours of the hen are not ſo bright and lively; her rump is green, back not ſo brown, and the belly not red, inclines to a
           dirty

dirty kind of green; the breast is also of a duller colour, more upon the grey.

The Time and Manner of building their Nest, &c.

THE Chaffinch breeds in May, and has young ones the beginning of that month. She builds near the top of an high hedge, or on the branches in the side of a tree: her nest is the prettiest of all small birds, excepting the Goldfinch's, which, I think, excels it in beauty: the outside is green moss, small sticks, withered grass, horse and cow hair, wool, feathers, &c. the inside lined with feathers, hair, wool, &c. making an exceeding soft bed for her young. The inside, or cavity of the nest, is an inch and three quarters deep; the diameter two inches and a half; and, notwithstanding the bottom and sides of this curious fabric were near an inch thick, the whole weight of a complete nest was no more than seven drams. Another nest, whose dimensions agreed with this, was two drams lighter. The bird itself, when fully grown, weighs about fourteen drams: its length, from the end of the bill to the end of the tail, is six inches; of which the latter is two and a half long. She lays usually four eggs, but

but sometimes five, of a whitish colour, spotted with a few large reddish brown spots, with a few small specks and streaks at the biggest end, of the same colour.

Of the Young, how to order them, &c.

THE Chaffinch has commonly but four young ones at a breeding; you may take them when they are about ten days old, and feed them as you do the Goldfinch or Linnet; they are hardy birds, that may be easily raised: and when they are out of order, apply the same things as you do to those birds when sick.

These birds are taken with clap-nets in great plenty, in June and July, especially the young flight, which we call Branchers, when they come to drink at their watering-place, &c. therefore 'tis hardly worth the trouble of bringing them from the nest, though some, that are bred under the sweet-song Chaffinch, sometimes prove very good birds.

Of

Green-Bird Cock, Hen and Egg.

Of the Greenfinch,

Green-linnet, *or, as it is commonly called, the* Green-bird.

The Deſcription and Character.

IT is a little bigger than the Chaffinch, of a ſtrong, hardy nature: they are frequently kept in cages, but not much eſteemed for ſinging; they are more valued for their learning to ring the bells in a cage contrived for that purpoſe: though ſome of them, if brought up from the neſt, will learn to pipe, whiſtle, and the ſong of moſt other birds.

At the beginning of winter, and in hard weather, they gather in flocks, and may be taken with the clap-nets in great numbers.

The Marks of the Cock and Hen.

HIS head and back are green, the edges of the feathers greyiſh; and the middle of the back hath ſomething of a cheſnut-colour intermixed: the fore-part of his head, neck, and breaſt, quite down to his belly and rump, are of a deep yellowiſh green;

green; the lower belly inclining to whitish: the borders of the outermost quill-feathers of the wings are of an elegant yellow; and the feathers along the ridge of the wing, are of a lovely yellow likewise. The colours of the hen are not so bright and lively; and on the breast and back hath oblong dusky spots: where the cock is of a fine yellow, her colours are of a sordid green. The young cock-birds, as soon as they are feathered, may be known from hens, by the same brightness in their colours.

The Time and Manner of their building.

THE Green-bird has young ones about the middle of May. She builds in hedges, and makes a large nest; the outmost part of which consists of hay, grass, stubble, &c.; the middle of moss; the inmost, on which the eggs lie, of feathers, wool, hair, &c. soft and pretty. She lays five or six eggs, of a very faint green colour, sprinkled with small reddish spots, especially at the blunt end. The inside was an inch and a quarter deep, and four wide; the whole composition weighed eleven drams; another nest I examined at the same time, differed not in weight quite half a dram, and had dimensions equal likewise. The bird, from the

end

end of his bill to the end of the tail, is fix inches and a half; the bill is half an inch; and the tail two and a quarter. Its weight is about fixteen drams.

Of the Young, how to order them, &c.

SHE has five or fix young ones at a breeding; they may be taken at ten days old, and brought up with the fame food and management as Linnets, or other birds of the Finch kind; they are not very tender: only keep them clean, and there is no fear but they will thrive. And after all, I cannot recommend them for pleafant cage-birds. If you regard his colours, he is as finely feathered as moſt birds; and in an aviary makes as pretty a fhow as the beſt of them.

He is feldom fick; but when he is, give him what you give Linnets or Chaffinches.

Of the common Linnet.

The Description and Character.

FOR the sweetness of its singing, the Linnet is so much esteemed, that by many persons he is thought to excel all small birds: he has certainly a curious fine note, little inferior to the best of birds; he may be taught likewise to pipe, whistle, or the song of any other fine bird; but as his own is so good, that trouble is unnecessary; the natural note of any fine song-bird, to my fancy, is ever to be preferred; but where the bird has but an indifferent song of his own, then to learn him to pipe, whistle, &c. is pleasant, and well worth the trouble. He is pretty apt in learning, if you bring him up from the nest, and will take the Wood-lark's song to perfection, or that of Canary-birds.

The Marks of the Cock and Hen.

YOU may know the cock-bird, either old or young, by these two marks; first, the feathers on his back are much browner than those of the hen; second, by the white of his wing. Take your Linnet, when the wing-

Linnet, Cock, Hen, & Egg.

wing-feathers are grown, and stretch out his wing, holding his body fast with the other hand, and then observe the white upon three or four feathers; if it appears clear and bright, and reaches up to the quills, it is a sure sign of a cock-bird; for the white in the wing of the hen is much less, and fainter.

The Time and Manner *of their building.*

THE Linnet has young ones by the end of April, or beginning of May; builds commonly in a thick bush or hedge; I have seen her in both black and white thorn; she likewise builds among furze-bushes, &c. making a small pretty nest: the outside of bents, dried weeds, and other stubby matter; and the bottom all matted together: the inside of fine soft wool, or cotton, mixed with downy stuff gathered from dried plants, with a few horse hairs, exceeding neat and warm. The cavity of this nest was one inch deep; diameter three inches, and the weight five drams. The nest here described, was taken with young ones in a furze, May the ninth. I believe the nest which the Linnet builds in a hedge, differs from this in the materials; I had not an opportunity now of examining both. She lays

lays either four or five white eggs, with fine red specks, especially at the blunt end. The bird, including the bill and tail, is five inches and a half long, of which the former is half an inch, the latter **two** and a quarter; in weight ten drams.

Of the Young, how to order them, &c.

THE Linnet has four or five young ones at a breeding; they may be taken at ten days old, or sooner; they will learn the song of another bird the better for being took young; but be sure to keep them very warm, and feed them once in two hours, from six in the morning, till six or seven at night: prepare their meat as was directed for the Bullfinch, viz. rape-seed soaked in water eight or ten hours; then scalded, strained, and bruised, mingled with an equal quantity of white bread, soaked in fair water, strained and boiled with a little milk, as I said before, to a thick consistency; let them have fresh every day, because sour meat will fling the birds into a scouring, which often brings death; when they begin to feed themselves, set scalded rape-seed in their cages, to wean them from the bread and milk as soon as possible, because, sometimes, feeding too long upon soft food, will make them rotten: it will

will be a month or six weeks before they will be able to crack their feeds, and live entirely upon hard meat. In the mean while, for change of diet, you may give them some of the Wood-lark's, or other birds victuals. There are other sorts of food made use of in bringing up young Linnets, but this is proved to answer as well as any.

The Linnet's *Diseases, and their Cures.*

THIS is a very healthful bird; I have known them kept many years without ailing any thing: but sometimes he is troubled with melancholy, occasioned from a swelling at the end of his rump, which, if ripe, you may with a needle let out the corruption, anoint the part with fresh butter, and feed him for two or three days with the seeds and leaves of lettice, or beets, or the seeds of melon chopt in pieces, which he will eat very greedily; and when you find him to mend, take the melon seeds, &c. away, and give him his old diet again: you may put into his water a blade of saffron, and white sugar-candy, for a week or more, till you perceive the bird to be entirely recovered.

The disease this bird is most troubled with, is a scouring, occasioned by bad seeds, and

many

many times for want of water. There are three sorts of this distemper; the first very thin, and with a black substance in the middle, which is not very dangerous. The second is between a black and a white, not so thin as the other, but very clammy and sticking; this is worse than the former. It is recovered by giving the bird some melon-seed shred; lettice-seeds, and beet-seeds bruised; and in his water put liquorice or saffron. The third and worst sort of scouring is the white clammy, which is dangerous and mortal, if not looked after in time. For this, give him first flax-seeds, taking away all other seeds; then give him plantain-seeds, if green, otherwise they will do him no good: for want of plaintain-seeds, give him some of the leaves shred small, or a little bruised hemp-seed; putting into his water, as before, sugar-candy, liquorice, or a blade or two of saffron: you may give the bird now and then a small matter of seeded chick-weed, and a little chalk. You must be diligent at the first to observe him when he is sick, that so he may have a stomach to eat: for this third and worst sort of scouring, if it be not taken at the first appearance, it immediately causeth him to droop, and in two or three days his stomach will be quite gone, and then all medicines are useless.

Linnets

ENGLISH SINGING-BIRDS.

Linnets are taken with clap-nets in June, July, and Auguſt; and likewiſe flight-birds about Michaelmas in great plenty, by laying the nets near where the birds come to drink, or feed; or upon any ſpot of ground they frequent.

As you catch the birds, put them into what you call a ſtore cage, made for that uſe, and give them ſome of the ſame feed you find them feeding upon, and put into the cage likewiſe fine hemp-feed bruiſed; feed them after this manner for two or three days, ſetting them where they will not be diſturbed, and they will ſoon grow tame; then you may cage them ſingle, in back cages, or any other, not too big; and feed them with rape and canary-feed, which agrees the beſt with them of any feed.

Of the Twite.

The Description and Character.

THE Twite is in colour and make something like the Linnet, but less; he has a very short bill, and dark, or blackish legs; the cock has a curious red spot upon his rump, which the hen hath not. 'Tis a bird vastly brisk and merry, that's always a singing, therefore they hang him among other birds, to provoke them to sing. They do not breed in England, that I know of, but come here in winter, and go away again in the spring; but what place they come from, or whither they go, to us is unknown: the bird-catchers take them as they do Linnets, &c. They eat rape and canary-feed, but love the canary best: 'tis a pretty, familiar, gentle-natured bird, well worth keeping.

I have been told by a gentleman, curious in such enquiries, that the Twite is common in some parts of France, and is called there by a name, which with us signifies the lesser Linnet; and that its egg is like the egg of that bird, but less.

The Twite, Cock, Hen, and Egg.

Sky-Lark, Cock, Hen and Egg.

Of the Sky-lark.

The Description and Character.

THE cock Sky-lark is as good a song-bird as most this land produces: he is vastly stout and lavish in his song; but thought by some people too loud and harsh. I must own, though he has a great many fine notes, they are not so melodious as the Wood-lark's, which in variety and softness much excels him, and, to my fancy, all small birds, without exception; but that valuable bird is exceeding tender, very subject to the cramp and other diseases, so that he can be kept but a short time in a cage; two or three years we count a great while. I don't deny but sometimes they reach beyond that date: yet the far greater number make their period a great deal sooner; whereas the Sky-lark is a long-lived, healthful bird, that will reach fifteen or twenty years; I have heard of several which have lived to that age, and sung stoutly all that time; therefore, considering the stateliness and beauty of this bird; his great freeness in singing his pleasant harmonious notes, for at least eight months in the year, and the time he may be kept in a cage, with care,

care, is highly deferving of the character I have given him, and worthy the efteem of all lovers of birds. If you can bring a young one up under fome fine Song-lark, 'tis a way to have a very valuable bird; but if you fuffer him to hear other birds, he will be apt to take their notes, whether good or bad, to which no bird is more fubject.

To know the Cock from the **Hen.**

TO diftinguifh one from the other in this kind, is no eafy matter; and about which there are various opinions, but hardly one that can be depended upon: they fay, the bird that fets up his feathers on his crown, is certainly a cock; and that the longeft heel bird is another fure fign; and fome fay, by two white feathers in the tail: this is all but guefs work, that fometimes proves right, and fometimes wrong. I am told, the biggeft and longeft bodied bird never fails of proving a cock; I can't fay that I ever made the obfervation myfelf, nor do I pretend to know a cock-bird of this kind till he is about a month old; when he will begin to record his notes very diftinctly, like an old bird, but low and inwardly; if you hear him do that, you can't well be deceived.

When

When they are grown up, and fully feathered, that general remark, in some measure, will hold good, that the highest-coloured bird is the cock; for whoever observes them together may perceive the Cock-lark to be something browner upon the back; of a more yellowish cast on the throat and breast, and the feathers whiter upon the belly.

The Time and Manner of building their Nest, &c.

THE Sky-lark has young ones by the end of April, or beginning of May. She builds her nest, such as it is, for she uses but very little stuff about it, only with a few bents, or such like materials, always upon the ground, or in a hole made by the foot of a horse, the wheel of a cart, &c. either in corn-fields of any sort, or in pasture of any kind; and lays four or five brown eggs, almost the colour of a clod of earth, thickly specked, as the figure represents, with brownish specks.

Of the Young, how to order them, &c.

THESE birds must be taken when about ten days old; if you let them alone longer,
you

you run a great hazard of losing them; I have known them quit their nest in seven or eight days, when they have been disturbed, especially if the old ones see you look at their young, they will then intice them away of a sudden; and in rainy weather, 'tis surprizing to see how young they will leave their nest; I have been disappointed at such a time, when I thought it almost impossible for them to get away: one would naturally think the nest to be the best and safest place for them in such weather; but so it is, I have remarked it often, that the young of most, if not all kinds of birds, are nourished more, their feathers grow faster, and they sooner fly, or quit their nests, in wet, than in dry weather.

When you have taken a nest of young, put them into a little basket with some short clean hay at the bottom, cover and tie them down close and warm, and feed them with white bread and milk boiled thick, mixed with about a third part of rape-seed, soaked, boiled and bruised: some bring them up with sheep's heart minced very fine, or other flesh meat. I cannot too often repeat the care that is necessary, in bringing up young birds, in keeping them clean, and feeding them regularly once in about two hours, from morning till night, with fresh and wholesome food, as the principal means of preserving them:

them: in a week's time you may cage them in a large cage, putting some hay cut pretty short, or coarse bran, at the bottom, turning or shifting it every day. Order them after this manner till they can feed themselves with dry meat, viz. bread, egg, and hemp-seed, which they will do in about three weeks or a month. Remember to boil your egg very hard, grate it fine, and mix it with an equal quantity of hemp-seed, bruised while the birds are young, but when they are able to crack the seed, give it them whole, and a little bread grated among it. You may then let them have a fresh turf of grass once or twice a week, and sift some fine dry gravel at the bottom of the cage, shifting it often, that it may not clog their feet: for change of diet, you may sometimes give them a little of the flesh meat. After they have done moulting, you may give them bread, egg, and whole hemp-seed every other day, and a fresh turf once a week. As the birds are of an hardy nature, this careful management will preserve them many years.

This bird at full growth is six inches and a quarter long; of which the tail is three inches, and the bill three quarters of an inch. When in flesh it weighs about an ounce and half.

The Sky-lark, as mentioned before, seldom ails any thing; but if you perceive him

at

at any time to scour, or dung loose, grate a small matter of old cheese among his victuals, or give him three or four wood-lice in a day, or a spider or two, and in his water a little saffron, or liquorice; **these are the best things that I can recommend, and what will relieve him;** though he won't often stand in need of any thing more than good meat and drink, clean gravel, and a fresh turf.

Several Ways of catching Sky-larks.

To take Pushers.

THEY are birds which have left their nest three or four days: to take them, **you** must watch in some convenient place, as much out of the old ones sight as possible; either stand close in a hedge, **or** lie down in the field, &c. and you will presently see them bring meat to feed their **young;** which, as soon as you perceive, **and observe them to hover just over the grass, &c.** and **drop down on a sudden, run** in upon them as fast **as you can, where you will** generally find the young birds; **if you miss them,** search narrowly about, **for they will creep** into some hole and lie close, or in a large turf of grass, &c.: sometimes they will run away among the grass or corn, exceed-

ing

ing faſt; when they do that, you can very ſeldom catch any: you muſt wait for the old ones bringing them meat again; **but don't run in the firſt time; ſee if they come two or three times with meat, and ſettle at the** ſame place; if at different places, **and** at little diſtances **from** each other, **then** you may be ſure the young ones have ſtraggled in the fright, and are at thoſe different places; you may then run in where **you** judge they are, by the conſtant coming **in of** the old birds, who will find them out, and ſoon **get** them together **again.**

When you take any of theſe **birds,** put them in a large cage with hay or coarſe bran at the bottom, and feed and order them as you do the neſtling. If you find them ſullen, that they won't eat, you muſt for a little while cram them with ſheep's heart, &c. they will ſoon come to. Theſe birds generally prove as good, or better, than thoſe raiſed from the neſt.

To take Branchers.

WE call all thoſe young **birds** by that name that were bred, and flew that year, about two or three months old, before they have moulted their neſtling feathers; what are taken at that age, before they begin to moult, are very good, little inferior to the neſtlings;

nestlings; but after they have moulted, or in moult when taken, seldom prove good birds.

The time for taking Branchers is in June or July, with a Hawk, and a net of about eleven or twelve yards long, and three or four broad, with a line run through the middle of it. There must be two persons, one to carry the Hawk, the other to take hold of one end of the line; and when you find where Larks lie, get as near to them as you can, then hold your Hawk up upon your hand, making him hover his wings, which when they perceive, they will lie very close to the ground: then let one take hold at one end of the line, and another hold of the other end, till you come at the place where they are, holding your Hawk up as you go; at the sight of which, they will lie so close that you may very easily draw your net over them. When you have taken them, give them bread, egg, and bruised hemp-seed; put in the bottom of the cage red sand, and strew them a little meat in the cage for two or three days, and they will presently become tame.

Sky-larks are taken in flight with clap-nets in great numbers. In some places they take them with a glass, called a Larking-glass; this they use of a sun-shiny day, which makes great havock amongst these birds: but

but the moſt deſtructive way is in the dark nights with a net called a Trammel; 'tis a very murdering net, taking all ſorts of birds that it comes near, as Partridges, Quails, &c. Larks are enſnared likewiſe with a nooſe made with two horſe-hairs twiſted together, which catches them by their neck or legs. This way is practiſed when the ground is covered with a deep ſnow.

Of the Wood-lark.

The Description and Character.

THIS bird is univerfally admired for his great variety of foft and delightful notes, that, in the opinion of moft people, he is the beft fong-bird found in this kingdom: he is not only, as fome have faid, comparable to the Nightingale for finging, but, in my judgment, deferving to be preferred before that excellent bird; and if he be hung in the fame room, will ftrive with him for the maftery; as likewife it fometimes happens in the woods, where there is a ftrong contention between thefe two chorifters to excel and outdo each other. If brought up from the neft, and caged in the fame room with a Nightingale, he will learn his notes, and as it were incorporate them with his own.

He is of great beauty, both in fhape and plume: his breaft and belly are of a pale yellowifh hair-colour, faintly fpotted with black; the back and head are party-coloured, of black and reddifh yellow, a white line encompaffing the head from eye to eye, like a crown or wreath. It is fomething leffer, and fhorter bodied than the common

Sky-

Wood-Lark, Cock, Hen, and Egg.

ENGLISH SINGING-BIRDS.

Sky-lark, and fits upon trees, which that bird seldom or never does.

In addition to Mr. Albin's account, the editor of this book takes the liberty of adding an account sent by a gentleman that has made many accurate observations on birds:—The cock Wood-lark is flat-headed, and full behind the ears, with a white stroke from each nostril, forming a curve-line over the eye, and almost meeting behind the neck; the whitness of this line, and its extension behind the neck, are the best signs to distinguish the male: they are full-chested, long from the neck to the shoulder of the wing, narrow on the vent and rump; the rump part a dark brown, with a long lightish tail, and the two corner feathers touched with white; long in body, and carries himself upright; some of the feathers under the throat have small stripes; they have three small white feathers on the top of the shoulder, and a long heel.

The hen is narrow-headed, and brown over the eyes, flattish from the breast to the belly, and round at the rump, short-heeled, and only two whitish, dull, or cream-coloured feathers on the shoulder, and the curve-line of the head reaches but a little beyond the eye.

The Marks of the Cock and Hen.

HE is known by his fize, the biggeft and longeft-bodied bird generally proving a cock; and by the largenefs and length of his call; the tall walking of the bird about the cage; and at evenings the doubling of his note, which we call cudling, as if he were going to rooft. Other marks are by the length of his heel, the largenefs of his wing, and by his fetting up the crown upon his head: fome will tell you, that thefe are certain figns of its being a cock; yet they do not always prove true: but if you hear him fing ftrong, you cannot be deceived, for the hen-bird will fing but little. The ufe of this is chiefly to know thofe birds that are taken at flight-time; becaufe thofe taken at other feafons, fing foon after they are taken, or not at all. I cannot give any certain notes to know the cock from the hen, whilft neft-lings; unlefs it be by that general remark, that the higheft-coloured bird always proves a cock, and that the biggeft, and longeft-bodied, and other marks before mentioned, will hold good in fuch young birds, as well as thofe that are full-feathered. This particular indeed is not very material, becaufe fo few are brought up from the neft; it being very difficult, with the utmoft care that can be taken, to raife them; either the cramp or scouring kills them; or they die in moulting.

The Time and Manner of their building, &c.

IT is a very tender bird, and yet breeds early in the spring, as soon as the Blackbird, or any other; the young birds being ready to fly by the middle of March. They build at the foot of a bush or a hedge, or in lays where the grass is rank and dry, under some turf to shelter them from the weather. Their nest is made of withered grass, fibrous roots, and other such like matter, with a few horse hairs withinside at the bottom, being a small, and very indifferent fabric; it has hardly any hollow or sides, the bottom was almost upon a level with the top: the whole composition did not weigh a quarter of an ounce: the weight of the bird a little above an ounce; its length six inches, of which the bill is something above half an inch, and the tail two inches. She lays four eggs, of a pale bloom-colour, beautifully mottled and clouded with red, yellow, &c.

Of the Young, how to order them, &c.

THE Wood-lark, as I said before, breeds very early in the spring; her young ones are tender

tender birds, and generally four in number: if you are minded to bring them up from the neft, which you will find exceeding difficult to do, don't take them too foon, not before they are well feathered; becaufe, when they are too young, they are more fubject to the cramp and fcouring, which commonly kills them: put them into a bafket with a little hay at the bottom, or fome fuch thing, where they may lie clean and warm, tying them clofe down: feed them with fheep's heart, or other lean flefh meat, raw, mixed with a hard-boiled egg, a little bread, and hemp-feed bruifed or ground, all chopped together as fine as it is poffible to do it, and made a little moift with clean water: every two hours, or oftner, give them five or fix fmall bits, taking great care never to overload their tender ftomachs. Let not their meat be too ftale, dry, mouldy, or four; for your birds fo fed, whether old or young, will never thrive.

The wild ones feed upon beetles, caterpillars, and other infects; likewife upon feeds.

The Wood-lark, as if fenfible of his own melodious fong, will take from no other, unlefs brought up from the neft; then he may be taught the fong of another bird.

The

The Seafons for catching Wood-larks *with Nets, and how to order them.*

FIRST, Branchers, which are birds that were hatched that fpring, are taken in June and July, with a net and a Hawk, after the fame manner as I told you they took Sky-larks. You may find thefe birds harbouring about gravel-pits, upon heath and common land, and in pafture fields. For fear of the Hawk, they will lie fo clofe, that fometimes they fuffer themfelves to be took up with the hand. Thefe birds foon grow tame.

The next feafon is for Michaelmas birds, which are taken with clap-nets in great numbers in September, and are counted better birds than what are catched at any other time of the year, becaufe keeping them all the winter, makes them more tame than birds catched in January or February, and will fing longer, eight or nine months in the year. Wood-larks, at this time, commonly fly very high, therefore the higheft ground is ufually chofe to lay the nets upon, likewife in a cart-way, or where a fpot of earth is frefh turned up; or fometimes you may turn it up on purpofe.

A third feafon for taking Wood-larks is in January; what are caught at that time, are very ftout, good birds, and will fing in a few days

days after they are taken, both stouter and louder than one taken in September, but not sing so many months: these are catched with the clap-net likewise, as they are at Michaelmas; and are found at that time of the year, lying near a wood-side in pasture ground, where the sun rises.

Wood-larks are sometimes taken when they are matched with their hen, which, I think, is wrong; they should by no means be disturbed in breeding-time, or when they are preparing for it: the end of January ought to be the latest time for taking these birds, because they are early-breeding birds, that, if the weather be mild, couple at that time, or soon after; besides, the bird taken then is worth very little; 'tis true, he will sing almost as soon as you have him, by reason of his rankness in accompanying with the hen, but will soon fall off from his song, and you hear but little more from him all that summer.

All the Wood-larks, taken at different seasons, must be fed alike with hemp-seed bruised very fine, and mixed with bread and egg hard boiled and grated, or chopped as small as possible. When he is first taken, he will be shy for a little time; you must sift fine red gravel in the bottom of his cage, and scatter some of his meat upon it, which will intice him to eat sooner than out of his trough;

One egg will serve six Woodlarks very well for two days.

trough; you may leave that off when you find he eats out of the latter freely.

In a great meafure, order his diet as the Sky-lark's; give him no turf of grafs, but often fine red gravel in his cage; and when not well, inftead of that, put mould full of ants, which is the moft agreeable live-food you can give him. Or give him meal-worms, or hog-lice, not more than two or three a day: and let him have a little faffron or liquorice fometimes in his water. If he fhould fcour, grate chalk or cheefe among his meat, and amongft his gravel likewife. He will eat any kind of flefh meat minced fine, and ordered as before for fome other birds; which you may now and then let him have for change of diet, always leaving fome of his conftant meat in the cage at the fame time, that he may eat which he will. A gentleman who is very fond of Wood-larks, keeps feveral, and among them one he has preferved for fix years, feeds them conftantly with a compofition of peafe-meal, honey, and butter, mixed, rubbed into fmall granules, and dried in a difh before a fire. Of this meat he makes enough at one time to ferve fix or eight birds for fix weeks or two months; which, if judicioufly mixed and dried, will not fpoil, even if kept longer.

An uncommon care ſhould be taken of preſerving this fine bird, becauſe he is ſo very tender, in often ſhifting his gravel, victuals, water, &c. and ſome think it neceſſary to wrap a piece of cloth round their perches in very cold weather.

Tit-Lark, Cock, Hen, & Egg.

Of the Tit-lark.

The Description and Character.

THIS bird is less than the Sky-lark, about the bigness of the Nightingale; very handsome shaped, and finely feathered; so that in beauty few birds excel him: he sings most like the Canary-bird of any whatsoever, whisking, curring, chewing, &c. but his song is short, and hath no variety in it. Sometimes indeed a cock Tit-lark proves a very fine song-bird, but 'tis very rare, and the best of them sing but four or five months in the year.

He comes with the Nightingale, about the end of March, and goes about the beginning of September. Before his going away, he is apt to grow fat like the Nightingale: he is a hardy bird, and long-lived; if preserved with care, not subject to colds or cramps.

The Marks of the Cock and Hen.

IN this kind the cock is all over more yellow than the hen, but especially under the throat, on the breast, legs, and soals of the feet. In nestlings, they can't well be distinguished by their colours, therefore must wait till you hear

hear them begin to record their song, which is the surest sign of a cock-bird.

Of their Nest, &c.

THE hen Tit-lark builds amongst grass, or in corn-fields; her nest is small, pretty much like the Wood-lark's: she lays five or six eggs of a dark-brown colour; and has young ones fit to take towards the end of May.

They may be brought up with the same meat and management as young Wood-larks or Nightingales: but I think it hardly worth the trouble, because so many are taken, when they first come to visit our part of the world, both with clap-nets and lime-twigs, as they catch Linnets, Goldfinches, &c. When you first take them, tie the ends of their wings with thread, to prevent their fluttering and beating themselves against the cage, and they will soon grow tame. Feed them as you do the Wood or Sky-lark: at first give them hemp-seed and bread, made very fine and mixed together; likewise ants mould in their cage, meal-worms, &c.; strew their victuals about their cage, to allure them to eat, and in three or four days they will take it freely enough; and will sing in about a week's time. Cage them single, in a cage something closer than the common Wood-lark's.

Robin-Red-Breast, Cock, Hen, and Egg.

Of the Robin Red-breast.

The Description and Character.

THIS bird, denominated from its red breast, is so well known in almost all countries, that it needs no long description. It is by many persons esteemed little inferior to the Nightingale; the cock has a sweet melodious song, so free and shrill, that very few birds can equal him.

In the winter-time, when there is a scarcity of meat abroad, the Robin, to seek its food, will enter into houses with much confidence, being a very bold bird, sociable and familiar with man: but in the summer, when there is plenty of food in the woods, and it is not pinched with cold, it will withdraw itself into the most desart places, being a solitary bird, that loves to feed singly; and lives upon worms and other insects, ants, and their eggs, crumbs of bread, &c. Notwithstanding these birds are said to withdraw from houses into the woods in summer-time, as indeed some of them do, yet are there a great many that breed and harbour about farm-yards and out-houses all the year round.

The Marks of the Cock and Hen.

THE cock may be known by his breaſt being of a deeper red than the hen's, and the red going up farther upon the head; and ſome ſay, by the colour of his legs, which are darker, and by certain hairs which grow on each ſide of his bill. His bright red breaſt is a mark that may be depended upon; the other do not always anſwer. The cock is likewiſe of a darker olive-colour upon the upper ſurface of his whole body.

The Time and Manner of building their Neſt, &c.

THE Robin has young ones by the end of April, or beginning of May. She builds in a barn or out-houſe; ſometimes in a bank or hedge; and likewiſe in the woods: her neſt is made with coarſe materials; the outſide of dry green moſs, intermixed with coarſe wool, ſmall dried ſticks, ſtraws, dried leaves, peelings from young trees, and other dried ſtuff; with a few horſe-hairs withinſide: it had a very little hollow, hardly an inch deep, and about three wide; the compleat neſt weighed eleven drams. Another, whoſe dimenſions were equal with this,

this, was half a dram lighter. The bird is fix inches long, of which the bill was little more than half an inch, and the tail two and a half long. She lays commonly either five or fix eggs, but fometimes no more than four, never lefs, of a cream-colour, fprinkled all over with fine reddifh yellow fpots; at the blunt end fo thick, that they appear almoft all in one.

Of the Young, how to order them, &c.

AT the beginning of May, the Robin ufually has young ones fit to take, five or fix in number: you may take them at ten or twelve days old: if you let them lie too long, they are apt to be fullen. Keep them warm in a little bafket, with hay at the bottom; feed them with the Wood-lark's meat, or as you bring up young Nightingales. Let their meat be minced very fmall, as ordered for other birds, giving them but little at a time; if you over-load their tender ftomachs, it will diforder the birds: when they are grown ftrong, cage them in a cage like the Nightingale's or Wood-lark's; it fhould be fomething clofer wiered, and let them have mofs at the bottom; and, in all refpects, keep and order them like the Nightingale: when they feed them-

themselves, you may try them with the Wood-lark's meat, because some of these birds like it better than the Nightingale's.

Of their Diseases and Cure.

THEY are very much subject to the cramp and giddiness; for the cure of the former, give them a meal-worm now and then; for the latter, six or seven earwigs in a week.

There are many kinds of insects that birds will eat greedily, and very probably would relieve them under maladies, could they be conveniently procured at all times, such as young, smooth caterpillars (a Robin will not touch a hairy one) some sorts of spiders, ants, &c.; but I know of no insect that is more innocent, or agrees better with birds in general, than the meal-worm, which may be had with little trouble at the meal-shops almost at any time. The earwig I do not approve of; that insect is armed in the tail with a pair of very sharp forceps, which it can clasp together, and may wound or hurt the bird. Above all, to prevent diseases, be sure to keep him clean and warm, taking care never to let him want water or wholesome food, and sometimes

times put a little saffron or liquorice in his water, which will make him chearful, long-winded, and help him very much in his song.

A young one brought up from the nest, may be taught to pipe or whistle finely; but I prefer his own natural song to those that are taught him, because it is an exceeding good one.

Robins are taken with lime-twigs, and likewise with the trap-cage; by this last, great numbers are ensnared.

An old bird, when he is caught, is apt to be sullen, and when you put him in a cage, will not sing; but a young cock-bird will sing in a few days. What birds you catch in your traps, feed and order them as you do the Nightingales, and with particular attention, or they will pine, and die with discontent at the close confinement of a cage.

Of the Red-pole.

The Description and Character.

THE Red-pole is a very small, but an exceeding pretty-feathered bird: the head and breast of the cock are of a fine red: the hen has a red head likewise, but not of so bright a colour; 'tis not a very fine bird for singing, but has a pretty chattering sort of a note; I can't call it very melodious, yet they are often kept in cages, and eat the same sort of seeds as the Linnet or Chaffinch. We are not sure that these birds build in England; they are found here in winter, but go away again in the spring. I never saw or heard of any of their nests being found; I rather believe they come to shun the cold, as the Aberdivine, Twite, and some other birds do. They are taken as they catch Linnets, Goldfinches, and other small birds. Mr. Willughby has not the Red-pole in his collection, described by that name, or any other that will exactly answer; but I believe it to be the same with what he calls the Lesser Redheaded Linnet; his description of that, agreeing in many particulars with this bird, which is as follows:—This, says he, is lesser than

Red-Pole, Cock, and Hen.

than the precedent, meaning the Greater Red-headed Linnet, which he makes lesser than the common, and will agree very well with the size of the Red-pole; the back coloured like the common Linnet; the forehead adorned with a remarkable shining red spot; the bill like that of the Great Red Linnet, but less; the breast red; the lower belly white; the prime feathers of the wings and tails dusky; the tail about two inches long, and something forked; the outmost borders of the wing and tail-feathers round are white; the legs and feet are dusky; the claws black and long, for the bigness of the bird, but the legs very short.

In this kind, the female also hath a spot on her head, but more dilute than that of the cock, and of a saffron colour.

Of the Red-ftart.

The Defcription, Character, and Marks of the Cock and Hen.

IT is a fmall bird, fomething leffer than the Robin red-breaft. The cock is very beautiful; his breaft, rump, and tail are of a fine red; the back, neck, and hind part of the head of a lead colour; the fore part of his head and throat of a jet black, and has a white mark upon his pole. The hen is a beautiful bird likewife, but partakes more of the colour of the Nightingale, with a red tail, fomething fainter than the cock's. The cock is known at all times from the hen, by his black head, that mark being peculiar to the male only. He fings fweetly, and has pretty notes, very pleafant to hear.

Of their Breeding; when to take, and how to order the Young, &c.

THESE birds breed in May, have young ones fit to take by the middle of that month. They build their nefts in the holes of old walls, trees, &c. Their eggs are like the

Hedge-

Redstart, Cock, Hen, and Egg.

Hedge-fparrow's, but of a paler blue, and not fo big.

This bird is faid to be of fo dogged and fullen a temper, that if taken when old, will not for fome days look at his meat; and when he feeds himfelf, will fometimes continue a whole month without finging; but if brought up young, they become gentle and tame; and with regard to her neft, they fay, fhe is the fhyeft of all birds; for if fhe perceives you to mind her when fhe is building, fhe will forfake what fhe hath begun; and if you touch an egg, never comes to her neft more; and if you touch the young ones, will either ftarve or throw them out of the neft, and break their necks, as Mr. Willughby fays he found by experience more than once.

The young are to be taken at ten days old, and are to be fed and ordered as the Nightingale or Robin red-breaft. Keep them warm, and they will fing in the night as well as in the day, and will learn to whiftle, and imitate other birds: when wild, it feeds upon infects, &c. like the Robin or Nightingale; and 'tis thought comes to us in fummer time, and goes away in the winter; of which matter I own myfelf ignorant.

Of the Common Wren.

The Description and Character.

EXCEPTING it be the Golden-crowned Wren, this is the smallest bird found in this kingdom; it weighs about three drams; its length, from the point of the bill to the end of the tail, is four inches and an half. He commonly creeps about hedges and holes, making but short flights, and if it be driven from the hedges, may easily be tired and run down. It will sit upon a barn or tree, &c. about a farmer's yard, where it mostly frequents, and sing exceeding fine; and being kept in a cage it will sing very sweetly, and with a higher and louder voice, than one would think for its strength and bigness, and is a very pleasing bird, that will sing a great many months in the year. Some persons have kept these birds a great while in a cage, and have had them sing as stout as if they were in the fields.

The Marks of the Cock and Hen.

THE cock is of a dark brown upon the head and back; his breast and belly whitish;

Wren, Cock Hen, and Egg.

ENGLISH SINGING-BIRDS. 71

the tail and wings are varied with a bright yellow, and blackish lines. The bird with the largest eye is generally thought to be a cock. The hen-bird is all over of a reddish brown colour, excepting the lines across her tail and wings, which are black and reddish. The difference in young birds can hardly be known till the cocks begin to record and sing.

The Time and Manner of their building, &c.

THE Wren has young ones in May; she builds her nest sometimes by the walls of houses, in the back-sides of stables, or other out-houses, but more commonly in woods and hedges, in a very artificial manner, having the form of a sugar-loaf; and about as large as a pint pot; without of moss, within of hair, wool, or feathers, and hath in the middle of the side a door or passage, by which it goes in and out; she lays a great number of eggs, sometimes fifteen or sixteen, but many times hatches not above half that number; they are very small white eggs, sprinkled all over with small pale red spots.

Of the Young, how to order them, &c.

IF you are minded to bring up a nest of Wrens, let them be very well feathered

before

before you take them: they are to be fed and reared like the young Nightingales, giving them often, and but little at a time, one or two very fmall bits. When they are grown fit for a cage, let them have a large one made with very clofe wire; one fide of which fhould be made like unto a fquirrel-houfe, and have it lined with any thing that is warm. Keep them conftantly to the Nightingale's food, and there is no queftion but they will anfwer your expectation; you muft take the fame care in keeping them clean and warm as of young Nightingales. And if at any time they are fick, give them two or three flies, or a fmall fpider or two, but not too many infects.

Nightingale; Cock, Hen, and Egg.

A Saxon word is said to form the etymology of the name, viz. galan, "to sing," combined with night, as the nightingale pours forth its strains in the lonely hours of repose. These vigils did not pass unnoticed by the ancients, who have remarked that "to have less sleep than a nightingale is a sign of a bad sleeper."

Of the Nightingale.

The Description and Character.

NOtwithstanding the particular fancy of divers persons for this or that bird, which they esteem and prefer to all others, the Nightingale, by the generality of mankind, is still accounted the chief of all singing-birds: he sends forth his pleasant notes with so lavish a freedom, that he makes even the woods to echo with his melodious voice; and this delightful bird, scorning to be out-done, will not yield to any competitor, either of birds or men; the Woodlark is his greatest antagonist, between whom there sometimes happens such a contention for mastery, each striving to outvy the other, that, like true-bred cocks, they seem resolved to die rather than lose the victory. If the former carries it in stoutness and freeness of song, so does the latter in his pleasing variety of soft warbling harmonious notes, in which, to my fancy, none excels, or is equal to him.

The Nightingale is not so remarkable for any variety or beauty of colours, but well known from its singing by night: in size he is about the bigness of the Goldfinch, something longer bodied.

These birds are not seen in this kingdom in the winter-time; where they are when absent from us, is altogether unknown: they come towards the latter end of March, or beginning of April, and leave us at the latter end of the summer. Those that are kept here in cages will sing seven or eight months in the year, from the beginning of November till midsummer: there must be a great deal of care taken to keep them clean and warm, and they will sing all the winter; a little time reconciles them to a cage, where they may be bred like Canary-birds.

The Marks of the Cock and Hen.

THERE are no particular marks in their colours to know them by; but as in other birds, so in these, the cock is of a deeper and brighter colour than the hen, which, when seen together, may easily be perceived, and is something larger. In nestlings the cock may be known by this token; after he hath eaten, he will get upon the perch, and begin to tune or record to himself, which you may observe by the motion of his throat; whereas the hen at first records little, or not at all. *If young ones are taken before they have learned their song from their parents, they will never sing so well as others.*

*The Time and Manner of building their Nest,
&c.*

THEY have young ones usually by the middle of May; build in a close, thick hedge, pretty low, a little above the edge of the bank, and most commonly where briars, thorns, bushes, and such like things grow very thick, to fence them from their enemies, making their nest of the leaves of trees, straws, and moss; and lay eggs of a brown nutmeg colour.

It seldom sings near its nest, for fear of discovering it, but, for the most part, about a stone's cast distant. It frequents cool and shady places, where are little rivulets of water, such as quickset hedges, small groves and bushes, where are no very high trees; for it delights in no high trees, except the oak.

To find the Nightingale's nest, observe where the cock sings, and if he sings long in a place, then the hen is not far off; but if he hath young ones, he will now and then be missing; and the hen, when you are near her nest, will sweet and cur; but if you have searched long, and cannot find it, try this experiment; stick two or three meal-worms upon the thorns, near where you find the cock most frequents, and stand still, or lie down close, keeping the worms in view, and obferve, when he comes to take them, which way he carries them: liften, and you will hear the young when the old ones feed them, for they make a great noife for fo fmall a bird. When you have found the neft, if they be not fledged enough, touch them not, if you do, they will not ftay long, the old ones will intice them out.

Of the Young, how to order them, &c.

THE Nightingale has five young ones at a breeding; they fhould not be taken till they are fledged almoft as well as the old ones; and though they are apt to be fullen, and refufe their meat, when they are fo old, you may open their mouths, and give them two or three fmall pieces at a time, and in a few days they will come to, and feed themfelves: if you take them too young, they are fubject to the cramp and loofenefs, which makes their feathers mat together, and kills the birds. When you take them, put the neft in a little bafket, and keep the birds covered up warm, for they are very tender, and without fuch care the cold will kill them. Feed them every two hours, giving them two or three fmall bits at a time: let their meat be fheep's heart, or other flefh meat raw, chopped very fine,
(well

(well cleansed and freed from skin, sinews, and fat or strings, which will be apt to stick in their throats, or twine about their tongues, and cause them to fall off from their meat, &c.) mixed with hens eggs hard boiled.

In a few days they will take their meat off from the stick themselves; you may then cage them in the Nightingale's back cage. Let them have a little straw or dry moss in the bottom of the cage; but when they come to be large, give them ants mould as you do the old ones: you may learn them to feed upon some kind of insects, such as meal-worms, spiders, ants, &c. being very useful when they are sick; I do not approve of giving them much of that sort of food when well.

Of the Nightingale's *Diseases, and their Cure*.

FIRST, note, that the principal thing which causes most diseases, not only in Nightingales, but in other birds kept for singing, is, as mentioned before, want of keeping them clean and neat, whereby they clog their feet, which causes the claws of several to rot off, and breeds the cramp and gout in others, and makes them never thrive,

thrive, nor delight in themselves. No birds can be kept too clean and neat, therefore be sure to let them have twice a week gravel at the bottom of the cage, and let it be very dry when you put it in, for then it will not be subject to clog.

In autumn this bird is apt to grow extraordinary fat and foggy, so that sometimes he will hardly touch his meat for a fortnight or more; during that time give him three times a week meal-worms, two or three at a time, or worms taken out of pigeon-houses, or two or three spiders a day, which will purge and cleanse him well. Upon the falling of his fat he must be kept warm, and have a little saffron in his water. To raise them when they are very lean and poor, give them figs chopped small among their meat, continuing no longer than till they have recovered their flesh.

When they have been kept two or three years in a cage, they are very subject to the gout; anoint their feet with fresh butter or capon's grease, three or four days together, and it is a certain cure for them. They are subject likewise to breakings-out about their eyes and nib, for which use the same.

If they grow melancholy, put into their water some white sugar-candy; if that will not

If you would secure a Nightingale in health, do not fail, in the month of March to purge him with half a dozen of black spiders, one every day.

not do, besides their constant meat of sheep's heart, &c. give them three or four meal-worms a day, and a few ants and ants eggs, and some of their mould at the bottom of the cage: also boil a new-laid egg, and chop it small, and strew it among the ants and their eggs; and let them have saffron in their water.

The Nightingale is sometimes troubled with a straitness or strangling of the breast, which comes very often for want of care in making his meat, by mincing fat therewith, or by reason of some sinew or thread of the sheep's heart, for want of well shredding, hanging in his throat, or clasping about his tongue, which causeth him to forsake his meat, and grow very poor in a short time; when you perceive this, which is known by the bird's gaping, and the unusual beating and panting of his breast, take him gently out of his cage, and open his bill with a quill, and unloosen any string or piece of flesh that may hang about his tongue or throat: after you have taken it away, give him some white sugar-candy in his water, or else dissolve it, and moisten his meat, which is a present remedy to any thing that is amiss. *There is an odd disorder which this is very liable to and may be called the falling sickness; after a precipitate motion he will drop from the perch on his back at once, with his legs stretched upwards, and his eyes distorted, when without speedy relief, he soon dies. The only remedy for this is to take him in your hands, and with a pair of scissars cut off his hinder claws so near to the heel as to draw a drop or two of blood; then wash the wound with warm water, of which, if he does not soon recover, make him swallow a drop warm, and he will be quite recovered in an hour or two.*

How to take Branchers *and old* Nightingales, *and to order them when taken.*

THE former are to be catched in July, or beginning of August, the latter at the end of March, or beginning of April; those taken in March, or before the 12th of April, are counted the best birds. What are catched after the 12th of that month, when the cocks are matched with the hens, by reason of their rankness, seldom come to any thing, it being very difficult to preserve them.

When you have found the birds haunts, which are usually in a wood, coppice, or quickset hedge, you may take them by the trap-cage, made on purpose for catching of Nightingales, baited with a meal-worm: place your trap as near where the bird sings as you can; if it is in the middle of the hedge, or a place where he used to feed, before you fix the trap, turn up the earth about twice the bigness of the trap; for where the ground is new turned up, there they look for food, and espying the worm they come presently to it; if they come not soon, then turn up a fresh spot of earth, as big again as the former, and you will quickly have them, for they will not leave the place where they use to resort. It is proper to this bird, as they say, at his first coming,

coming, to settle, or seize upon one place as its freehold, into which it will not admit any other Nightingale but its mate.

These birds are taken likewise with lime-twigs, by placing them upon the hedge, near where they sing, with meal-worms fastened at proper places, to allure them to the snare; but I think the trap-cage is a great deal the best way of catching them.

As soon as you have taken one, tie the tips of his wings with some thread, not straining it too hard, to prevent his beating himself against the top and wires of the cage; he will grow tame the sooner for it, and be more apt to eat his meat. You should put him in a Nightingale's back cage; or if an open one, darken one side with cloth or paper; and at first hang him in some private place, that he be not disturbed. Feed him once in an hour and half, or two hours, with sheep's heart and egg shred small and fine, mingling amongst the same some ants, or meal-worms. And because no Nightingale will at first eat any sheep's heart or egg, but must be brought to it by degrees; his food being live meat, as worms, ants, caterpillars, or flies; therefore, taking the bird in your hand, you must open his bill with a stick made thin at one end, and give him three, four, or five pieces, according as he takes them, as big as peas; then set him some meat mingled with store of ants, that when he goes to pick up the ants, he may eat some of the heart and egg with it: at the first you may shred three or four meal-worms in his meat, the better to intice him, that so he may eat some of the sheep's heart by little and little, and when you perceive him to eat freely, give him the less ants, &c. in his meat, and at last, nothing but sheep's heart and egg. You should take some of this meat with you when you go to catch Nightingales, and in an hour or two after they are taken, you must force them to eat, by opening their mouth and cramming them, taking care that their meat be not too dry; moisten it by sprinkling a little clean water upon it, as you prepare it. Remember, when you first take a bird, to clear his vent from feathers, by pulling, or cutting them off, otherwise he will be subject to clog and bake up his vent, which is sudden death. Birds that are long a feeding, and make no curring or sweeting for eight or ten days, seldom prove good; but on the contrary, they give great hopes of proving well when they take their meat kindly, and are familiar, and not buckish, and sing quickly, and learn to eat of themselves without much trouble. This is a sure token of their proving.

ENGLISH SINGING-BIRDS.

proving excellent birds: when they will feed in a few hours, or the next day after they are taken, and sing in two or three days; those never prove bad. You must tie the wings of the bird no longer than till he is grown tame. *To bring up young Nightingales.*

Get a nest of the first layer, as being the most vigorous and stout birds, consequently the best singers, and the least liable to fail in moulting. You must not take the nest till the birds are pretty strong, and when taken they should be carried home in a dark basket with a few breathing holes. It is a nice point to feed them properly; too much or too little is dangerous. Their gaping wide is no indication that they want victuals, for this they will do whenever you come nigh them; about an hour after sun rising give them their first feed, the second an hour after, and so on till sun-set; give them four mouthfuls at a time, at a mouthful end if they are of the first lay, they will be able to feed themselves, which you may know by presenting them a small meal worm, you may then separate them in different cages. Another way. Take a nest of young ones, and place them in the same room with an old Nightingale. Begin to feed the young ones with the shower, and leave the old ones cage open day and night, taking care to place a small pot of the young ones meat close to his own feeding-trough: if you suffer the young ones to cry a little while, before you go to feed them, you will soon perceive the old bird go out of his cage, chirp to the young ones, fill his bill with their meat, and feed them; then in the morning, you find that he has been distributing meat to the young ones, you may entirely entrust him with that business; for when once he has undertaken it, he will

Of the Red-Grosbeak.

Of the Virginia-Nightingale, *called likewise, the* Red-bird.

The Description and Character.

IT is near as big as the common Song-thrush: the basis of his bill is encompassed with a border of black feathers reaching to the eyes: it hath a large head, adorned with a high towering crest, of a bright scarlet colour, as is also the whole bird, except the back, some part of the wings, and the tail, which are of a more dirty and brownish red. These birds are brought from Virginia, New England, and other parts of North America, where they catch them as we do Larks in England, by sweeping away the snow, and baiting the place with Virginia wheat, &c. It hath an agreeable melodious song, with some notes like the English Nightingale. The hen is not so beautiful as the cock, being more brown, with a tincture of red: these sing when in cages, as well as the cocks, and are brought over with them.

Its strength with its bill is surprizing, it being able to crack the stones of almonds, olives,

Virginia Nightingale, Cock and Hen.

P. 84.

The Virginian Nightingale upon seeing itself in a glass has strange gesticulations, making a hissing noise, lowering its crest, setting up its tail like a peacock, shaking its wings, and striking at the looking glass with its bill.

Proper food for a Nightingale.

All meat agrees with a Nightingale, provided it is mixed with flesh; without which he will not be nourished. He is naturally inclined to feed and live on spiders, wood-lice, ants eggs, flies, and worms, which agree with his constitution: this has put many upon preparing compositions proper to be substituted in the room of his natural food. The most common is an equal part of hempseed, a little parsley, crumb of bread, and minced boiled fresh beef, well mixed together; this agrees very well with them, they may in time be entirely weaned from this food, and may be fed with German paste. When he is first caught you must put two cups into his cage one for water into which strew three or four meal worms; in the other twenty or thirty meal worms, for his food

ENGLISH SINGING-BIRDS. 85

olives, and Indian maize, very expeditiously, the kernels of which it is very fond of: in England they feed upon maize bruised, rice in the husk, wheat, barley, hemp, or canary-seeds; it will eat also the Wood-lark's, or Nightingale's food. There are persons with us that highly value these birds, which makes them sometimes sell at a great price. I have heard of those that have attempted to breed them in England, but made little of it. If your bird should be sick, a spider or meal-worm will relieve him.

Cardinal Grosbeak has attained the name of Virginia Nightingale from the fineness of its song, the notes of which resembles that of the Nightingale. In spring, and in most part of Summer, it sits on the tops of the highest trees, singing early in the morning, and piercing the ear with its loud pipe. These birds are kept in cages, in which they sing throughout the year, with only short intervals. They are fond of maize and buck-wheat; and will get together great hoards of those often as much as a bushel. They are also fond of bees. They are pretty tame, frequently hopping before the traveller. From their being familiar birds, attempts have been made to breed them in cages, but without success.

Of the Yellow-hammer.

The Description and Character.

IT is equal to the Chaffinch in bigness: both cock and hen are beautiful birds; and the cock will sing very prettily, when in the fields, but is not kept very common in a cage; yet he is no contemptible bird; besides his song, his fine feathers are enough to recommend him: a lovely yellow adorns his head, throat, breast, and belly; his back and wings are pretty much like the Linnet's. The hen is of a paler colour all over her body, and the parts that are of a fine yellow in the cock, in the hen are of a dirty green.

These birds build upon the ground, at the side of a river, pond, or brook; they make a large, flat, ordinary nest, with moss, dried roots of grass, weeds, &c. with horse-hair intermixed; more of the latter than I ever observed any other bird to make use of. She lays six or seven white eggs, veined and spotted with black. Her young ones are usually fit to take by the beginning of May; you may let then be ten or twelve days old before you take them. Feed them with flesh meat minced very fine, as you

prepare

Yellow-hammer, Cock, Hen, and Egg.

prepare it for other fmall birds; or you may bring them up with the Tit or Woodlark's meat; they will eat likewife worms cut in fmall pieces, which food agrees very well with them.

Thefe birds are common every where in England; for the moſt part, they abide on the ground, feeking their food there, of worms, feeds, and other things.

Of the Reed-sparrow.

The Description and Character.

THIS bird in bigness is equal to the Chaffinch: the cock has a black head and throat: a ring of white encompasses the neck: his breast and belly are white, spotted with reddish-brown spots: the back of a dusky brown, with black spots: the pinion of his wing is of a reddish colour; the rest of the wing and the tail, are of a dark brown: the hen, as in most birds, is not so fair coloured: the ring about her neck is darker, and scarce appearing, and her head is not black like the cock's.

They frequent the reeds by the rivers sides, where they breed, hanging their nests between the reeds; they are chearful, merry birds, and sing finely. When we walk in summer-time by the sides of the river, they generally afford an agreeable harmony. They are not kept very common in cages, therefore 'tis not necessary to dwell any longer upon this bird. Her eggs in colour are like the Hedge-sparrow's.

Reed-Sparrow, Cock, Hen & Egg.

Hedge-Sparrow, Cock, Hen, & Egg.

Of the Hedge-sparrow.

The Description and Character.

HE is about the size of the Robin red-breast; has a pretty long slender bill, of a dusky or blackish colour: the upper side of his body is party-coloured, of black, and dirty red; and his breast of a blue, or lead colour. This bird is as well known as any of our small birds, being found almost in every bush, so that hardly a boy who searches the hedges, but can give an account of its nest, eggs, &c. therefore it would seem unnecessary for me to take any notice of it, but that I think the Hedge-sparrow too much neglected: no bird is more despised. I am sure he ought to be more valued; he is a very pleasant song-bird, sings sweetly, and has a great variety of pretty notes: I have known them kept in cages by some curious persons, and much valued for their fine singing; a great many people cage worse, and account them good birds: 'tis plenty that lessens the worth of this bird, as of every thing else, though ever so valuable in itself. The hen is known from the cock, by a fainter breast, and being of a brighter colour on the back.

Of their building, &c. Their Young, and how to order them.

THESE birds, as I said before, build their nest almost in every hedge, low, and open, that it may be found with little difficulty. It consists chiefly of fine green moss, platted with a little wool and hair; 'tis not of so curious a model as some are. The hen **lays** commonly five eggs, of a fine pale blue, or sea-green colour. She has young ones at the end of April or beginning of May: take them at nine or ten days old, and feed them with bread and flesh meat, chopped very fine, and mixed together, made moist, as for other birds: or you may bring them up with the Wood-lark's victuals.

If the cock is brought up under some fine song-bird, he will take his song, and answer your expectation.

Sparrows have been considered by narrow minded men as destructive, useless animals, and Nature has been injuriously taxed with creating them for the sole intent of destroying other useful productions, without answering in themselves any one good and useful purpose. Even Buffon has depicted the sparrow as a bird that is extremely destructive, its plumage entirely useless, its flesh indifferent food, its notes grating to the ear, and its familiarity and petulance disgusting. We shall however sufficiently satisfy ourselves of the error of such impious declaimers, if we do but examine some of the propensities of these birds. The Sparrow, amply repays the husbandman and gardener for his petty thefts, by destroying innumerable insects. It has been calculated from actual observation, that a single pair of Sparrows, during the time of feeding their young, will destroy about four thousand caterpillars weekly; only consider, then, what millions of these pernicious insects are destroyed annually by one species of bird. We can hardly doubt but that the total extinction of the race of Sparrows, provided the breed of other birds of such habits was not increased, would soon prove the cause of an universal dearth. — Every caterpillar, whose life was thus preserved, would, when arrived to its perfect winged state, lay several hundred eggs, which immense increase of all the various caterpillars, that the Sparrow is known to search for and devour, would in a few years be equal to the destruction of every blade of grass, and every leaf.

    Extract from Bewick.

"Let us not condemn a whole species of animals, because in some instances we have found them troublesome or inconvenient. Of this we are sufficiently sensible; but the uses to which they are subservient in the grand economical distribution of nature, we cannot so easily ascertain. We have already observed that, in the destruction of caterpillars, Sparrows are eminently serviceable to vegetation, and in this respect alone, there is reason to suppose, sufficiently repays the destruction they make in the produce of the garden or the field. The great tables of nature is

Aberdevine, Cock, and Hen.

spread alike to all, and is amply stored with every
thing necessary for the support of the various fami-
lies of the earth: it is owing to the superior
intelligence and industry of man, that he is ena-
-bled to appropriate so large a portion of the best
gifts of Providence for his own subsistence and support.
Let him not think it waste, that, in some instances,

# ENGLISH SINGING-BIRDS.

Of the Aberdivine.

The Description and Character.

IN size and colour, it is pretty much like the Canary-bird, only the cock has a black spot upon his head, and a little black under his throat. The hen is more upon the grey, and has a spotted breast and belly. They are lively, merry birds, and sing very prettily, and are frequently kept in cages.

These birds do not breed any where in England that ever I heard of, but shift places according to the season of the year; they visit our parts in the winter-time, and leave us in the spring. They frequent the alder-trees, &c. by the river-side: the bird-catchers take them up as they do Linnets, Goldfinches, &c. and feed them like those birds. It is of a very mild nature, and not at all crafty, so that it is easily taken by any kind of engine or deceit.

Mr. Willughby calls it Siskin. It is, says he, kept in cages for its singing, and is common in Germany and England. At Vienna, in Austria, they call it Seisel, a name not much different from our English Siskin. In Sussex it is known by the name of Barley-bird, so called because it comes to them in barley seed-time.

Of the Canary-bird.

The Description and Character.

THIS bird has its name from Canaria, an island of the Atlantic sea; one of those which the ancients, for the excellent temperature of the air, called Fortunate; all those islands which they so named, being now called the Canaries; from whence these birds were first brought into Europe, and from no other place. Canary-birds are bred in large quantities, both for sale and amusement, in Germany, France, and England; and in each of those countries they have, by care, much improved the breed, beyond those now imported from the natural climate. Those brought from Germany are the least valued, because the suffocating heat of the stoves, generally used to warm the houses, in that country, renders the birds bred there tender, and short-lived: German birds seldom living above a year or two in this country.

The cock of this kind hath a very sweet and shrill note, which, at one breath, continued a long time without intermission, it can draw out sometimes in length, sometimes raise very high, by a various, musical inflexion

Canary-Bird Cock, Hen, and Egg.

inflexion of its voice, making very pleasant melody.

The Marks of the Cock and Hen.

AT proper times of the year, the cock Canary-bird discovers himself sufficiently by his vociferation; but the cocks and hens have so close a resemblance in feathers, that they are not easily distinguishable by sight, without some degree of experience: the marks described as pointing out the cock, being sometimes very equivocal. There are however tokens of a cock-bird, that an accurate eye may consult with advantage; and these are, that the fore-part of his head, his throat, pinion of the wing, and rump, are of a brighter yellow than in the hen: which marks will hold good, let the birds be of what sort they will. They always have a little yellow above their bills, under their throats, &c. of a strong deep yellow in the cock; in the hen of a much paler colour. There is a difference likewise in their vents; if you blow the feathers in both, you may perceive his to appear longer than that of the hen's.

Another mark of a male-bird is his size; the biggest and longest-bodied bird seldom fails of proving a cock; especially if his
gesture

gesture and carriage be sprightly and majestic; and if he often extends his neck and head with life and **vigour, then** you may depend upon its being a **cock-bird.** Besides all this, you may know him by his fine singing, in which you can't well be deceived; for if the hens attempt to sing, it is so indifferently, that 'tis not deserving of the **name** of a song; and whenever the cock sings, if you observe his throat, you will **see it swell** and play all the time he is warbling **out** his pretty notes. But let the hen sing well or ill, this motion is never observed in her throat. This one circumstance will be sufficient to direct you to choose a cock-bird at all times; when you will find, for the generality, all the other marks to correspond likewise.

Directions for choosing a Canary-bird; *and to know if he be in Health.*

THERE are two distinct species of Canary-birds known among **breeders,** besides some varieties under each, which latter are not material to enter into. These are, those birds which are all yellow, and those which are mottled, with a yellow crown: the former, in the breeding stile, being called *gay* birds, and the latter, *fancy* birds.

The

The fancy breed are esteemed the strongest, and have the boldest song, yet sometimes the difference of their voice is not very observable. Careless breeders will often match a gay bird with a fancy bird, and then the produce, partaking of both kinds, are called *mules*; being foul, irregular birds, of no value for feather, though they may prove as good as any, merely for singing. The choice of birds for breeding, will be considered under the next article.

For health, take a bird that appears with life and boldness, standing like a Sparrow-hawk, not subject to be scared at every thing that stirs: therefore, when you observe him, approach not too near the cage, lest by a motion of the hand, or otherwise, you disturb him: it will make the bird, though not well, appear sprightly, and in health for a little time; but if you stand quiet, and at a proper distance, you may soon discover whether it is the effect of surprize, or the natural spirit of the bird: if he stands up boldly, without crouching or shrinking his feathers: if his eyes look chearful, and not drowsy, they are good signs of a healthful bird: but on the contrary, if he be apt to clap his head under his wing, and stand all of an heap, you may be sure he is not well.

Observe

Obferve likewife his dung; which, when he is in perfect health, will be round and hard, with a fine white on the outfide, and dark within, and will quickly be dry. If he bolts his tail like a Nightingale, after he hath dunged; or if his dung be very thin, or of a flimy white, with no blacknefs in it, you may conclude he is a fick bird.

The next thing we are to regard in choofing a Canary-bird, is the goodnefs of his fong. Some of thefe birds will open with the fweet of the Nightingale, and run through feveral of that bird's fine notes, and end in the Tit-lark's fong; and fome will fing only the Tit-lark's. Others will begin almoft like a Sky-lark, and by a foft, melodious turn of the voice, fall into the Nightingale's fweet and jug, whifking and chewing after a very delightful manner. The birds that have fuch a curious change of harmonious notes, want no recommendations, every body muft be fenfible that they are valuable. There are others of this kind, that fing with fo much force, they even deafen the ears of the hearers with their fhrillnefs; many perfons are delighted with this kind of finging, others are offended at it. Therefore, before you purchafe the bird, hear him fing in a fingle cage; and as you have directions to know

know a cock-bird, and when he is in health, as to the colour and song, please your own fancy. *Of the whole species the Cine or green canary has the strongest pipe.*

To order them in Breeding, &c.

If you propose to breed gay birds, choose your cock and hen of a clear uniform yellow colour, without being spotted with foul feathers; for these foulnesses indicate a mixture in their blood, and that the breed has some time or other been crossed.

Breeders of fancy birds are still more curious as to feather; there being several subscription societies in London, which raise annual premiums for the finest birds, and who have a pattern bird beautifully engraved and coloured, as the standard of perfection; with his various characters explained in a technical stile underneath. But as a person ought to be a connoisseur before he undertakes to raise prize birds, it may be sufficient to observe, that no excellence in the feathers of fancy birds is any security for breeding equally perfect young ones from them; as defects will often appear in some respect or other: while on the contrary, two indifferent birds may sometimes produce a very fine one. The principal test of a good fancy bird, is the having a clean

H cap;

cap; that is, the crown of his head, defined by a horizontal line at the level of his eyes and beak, is to be of a clean yellow or white, without being broke or spotted with foul feathers; and a single feather of this kind, is a drawback from his perfection: though this degree of perfection is seldom found. Add to this, that his back, wings, and tail, ought to be as clear from yellow or white feathers. The finer he is mottled on the back, and clearer yellow he is on the belly, the handsomer he will be esteemed.

These general characters are equally requisite in the hen as in the cock; beside which the breeder is to be informed of a casual variety in fancy birds, which are all distinguished either as *mealies* or *junks:* the meally-birds being those whose crown and bellies are of a clear white or pale yellow; and the junks, whose crown and bellies are of a deep yellow. It is a standing rule among good breeders, never to match two meally or two junk birds together; and skilful bird-fanciers will decide at once upon a bird so bred.

The Canary-bird is a gentle, familiar animal, and will breed very kindly under due management: that is, if they are provided with convenient cages, proper necessaries, are kept clean, and are not interrupted
from

from time to time by the prying eyes of impertinent curiosity, or officious care. The hazards of their own mismanagement, admitting of no comparison with the dangers they are exposed to from over-nursing. In short, the best general rule that can be given, is to supply them with every necessary at due times, and then to interfere as little as possible in their domestic œconomy. The hens generally sit four times in a season; but if a hen sits upon a due number of eggs three times, she should not be permitted to build again, without she appears yet strong and hearty, for they will sometimes die on the fourth nest during laying, or fall so weak as not to compleat the sitting.

About the beginning of March, if the spring be mild, or later in proportion to its severity, you may put your birds together in their breeding-cage; and the larger it is, the more convenient it will be for the birds to exercise themselves: the common-sized cages being too small for the purpose. If you breed with several pairs flying loose in a room, it will be necessary to pair them in small cages for a fortnight or so, that they may contract a familiarity and attachment, before they are turned out promiscuously. Never attempt to breed with two hens in one cage, for their jealousy of each other will disappoint your expectations from both. There should be two nest boxes in every cage; for though the young ones generally leave the nest in fourteen days, the hen sometimes begins another nest before they are out; and if she has not a box provided, will build upon the young birds and smother them.

It may not be amiss also, as the hen is commonly attached to that corner of the cage where she first sits, to slide the nest of young birds farther in, when she inclines to build again, and put the empty box upon the spot from whence the nest is removed.

As soon as your birds are put together, you must begin to feed them with hard egg, and bread grated and mixed together. This should be given fresh every day, in the proportion of half an egg, with about three or four times the same quantity of bread, to every pair, throughout the season, beside their ordinary diet of rape and canary-seed. With this, they should also have a due supply of chick-weed, groundsel, plantain, or cos-lettice leaves, as the season affords; and a pan of clean water to wash themselves in at pleasure. The cage-makers supply all the proper furniture for these occasions

I would recommend to such persons as breed only a few birds for their diversion, to use

use large cages, it being much the best way: but these cages must always stand in one place; for if they are shifted about, the birds will never settle to their business. Those who intend to breed a number, should prepare a room for that purpose.

Let the situation of it, if possible, be such, that the birds may enjoy the benefit of the morning sun, which is both delightful and nourishing; and let the windows be covered with wire-work, that they may have the advantage of the air in good weather, which will make them thrive the better: keep the floor of the room clean, sometimes sifting fine dry gravel or sand upon it, and often removing the dung and other foul stuff. You must take care to fix nest-boxes, and back-cages, in every convenient corner and place of the room, at least twice the number that you have birds, that they may have the more variety to chuse a lodging to their minds; for some love to build high, and some very low, some in a light place, and others will chuse a dark place.

There ought to be two windows in the room, one at each end, and several perches at proper distances for the birds to settle upon, as they fly backwards and forwards. You may set likewise a tree in some convenient place of the room, to divert the birds, and some of them will like to build in it: you must observe that their nest is secure from falling through, **and if** in danger, **to tie the** tree closer to prevent it, and they will hatch there as well as in any other place. Remember, not to **put too** many birds together, eight or ten pair are enough for **a** middling room.

When your **birds are first paired,** as I directed before, turn them into this **room;** where they will live, as it were, a conjugal life; and notwithstanding there are several other birds in the same room, one cock and one hen, as they first coupled together, will keep constant to each other, and both concur and assist in sitting and feeding **their** young: for the cock-bird takes his turn in building the nest, sitting upon the eggs, **and** feeding the young, as well as **the hen.**

Of their Nest, and how to order the Young.

YOU must furnish the birds **with stuff** for making their **nest; such as** fine hay, elk's hair, and moss: but give them no wool or cotton; for their feet are apt to tangle in it, so that when they get off the nest, they are in danger of dragging it out after them. Let all these materials be thoroughly dry; then mix and tie them up together in a net,

ENGLISH SINGING-BIRDS. 103

or put them in a rack, so that the birds may easily pull it out as they want it; and let it be hung in proper places in the room for that purpose.

They build a pretty neat nest, about which they will sometimes be so industrious, as to begin and finish it in one day, though they are generally two or three days in making their nest. The hen lays commonly four eggs; and sits thirteen days.

When the young are hatched, leave them to the care of the old ones to nurse and bring up, till they can fly and feed themselves. The hen, as I said before, will sometimes build again before the former brood can shift for themselves; the care of which, she transfers to the cock-bird, who will feed and nurse them himself, supplying the care of both parents, while she brings on and attends her new progeny.

When the young Canary-birds can feed themselves, take them from the old ones, and cage them. If they are flying about the room, you may catch them with a small hoop-net at the end of a long handle, made for that purpose. They may soon be weaned from their soft meat to seed and greens. *At moulting time put a bit of steel not iron into their water changing it three times a week give them no other medicine, but a little more hempseed than usual.*

Of the Canary-bird's *Diseases* and their Cure.

BESIDES their moulting, which is common to all birds, they are subject to the following disorders. The first is a surfeit, occasioned either by a violent cold, or from eating too greedily upon greens, especially a rank sort of chick-weed with broad leaves, and without seeds, which is hurtful both to old and young birds, it being very apt to surfeit the latter. To discover when the bird has this distemper, blow the feathers on the belly, and you will perceive it swelled, transparent, and full of little red veins, (all its little bowels sinking down to the extreme parts of its body) and if far gone, black, which generally brings death. The cure of this disease, if taken in time, is to keep him warm, and give him whole oatmeal amongst his feed for three or four days, in order to cleanse him; and put liquorice in his water; but if he is too loose, instead of oatmeal, give him maw-seed and bruised hemp-seed, being more binding; and at the same time let him have a little saffron in his water; or you may boil milk and bread, with a little maw-seed in it; 'tis very good for the bird at such a time.

Another malady the Canary-bird is troubled with, is a little pimple on his rump, called the pip; it will generally go away of itself, but if at any time it is bad, and will not, when it is ripe, let out the fickly matter with the point of a fine needle, fqueezing it all out with as much gentlenefs as you can; after, take a bit of loaf-fugar, moiften it in your mouth, and put it on the fore, which will heal it.

A third difeafe is a kind of yellow fcabs that come about their head and eyes, which fometimes fwell, and are full of matter; anoint thofe places with frefh butter or lard, or the oil of fweet almonds; thofe things will cure it, unlefs it fpread, then nothing but time and cooling food will carry it off.

Canary-birds are fometimes feized with fits, and drop from their perches to the ground, where they tumble in convulfions. In this cafe, if they are difcovered in time, and plunged in a pan of cold water, they will generally recover.

The laft thing that I fhall take notice of is his moulting. You may know when this comes on by the bird's appearing rough, melancholy, and often fleeping in the day with his head under his wings; and the cage being covered with down and fmall feathers; for the young ones, the firft year, caft only their down and small feathers, and the second, their tail and wing-feathers.

Careful nursing is the principal means to preserve birds under this natural malady; therefore be sure to keep him warm; set him sometimes in the sun, when it shines powerfully, to bask himself, it will comfort him very much, always taking care to keep him from cold or wind, which are very prejudicial to him at such a time; let him have good nourishing food, beside his common seed; as scalded bread with the water squeezed out, and maw-seed: you may also put a little saffron in his water. If the weather is very hot when the birds are in their moult, give them liquorice in their water instead of saffron, and plantain or lettice-seed; but not any of that meat if it be cold weather.

In the winter-time, when green meat is not to be had, or the season is too cold to allow it, a little scalded bread, with the water squeezed from it, will be an agreeable regale to your birds once a week, and keep their bodies from being too much bound up, by their dry feed. A slice of a ripe apple or pear, now and then stuck between the bars of their cage, is also a feast that their songs will thank you for.

These things, with good attendance, will at all times contribute very much to the relief

lief of sick birds. And whatever else is delivered in this treatise concerning the nature, song, marks of male and female, building, breeding, feeding, &c. of birds, being founded upon experience, will upon trial answer likewise.

A method of preserving Birds with their elegant plumes unhurt —

Open the vent from the lower part of the breast bone down to the Anus, with a pair of scissors, and then extract all the contents; fill the cavity immediately with the following mixture. Take of common salt one pound, alum powdered four ounces, bring the lips of the wound together by suture, so as to prevent the stuffing from falling out. Open the head near the root of the tongue with the scissors, and after having turned them round three or four times, to destroy the structure of the brain fill the cavity with the mixture — as for the wings and thighs you must ——— *them for the salt in a few days will penetrate to those parts and preserve them equally with the body, hang the bird up*

INDEX.

ABERDIVINE, description and character, **page** 91

BLACK-BIRD, description and character, page 1. Marks of the cock and hen, 2. The building her nest, laying her eggs, &c. 3. Of their young, and how to order them; their diseases, and cure; 4.

Bullfinch, description and character; their food when wild; page 16. Marks of the cock and hen, 17. The time and manner of their building; of the young, and how to order them; 18.

CANARY-BIRD, description and character, page 92. Marks of the cock and hen, 93. Directions for choosing a Canary-bird, and how to know if he be in health, 94. Difference of their song, 96. How to order them in breeding, 97. When to match your birds, and to prepare a cage for breeding, 99; or to fit a room for the same purpose, 101. What stuff to furnish them with for their nest, 101. How to order their young, 102. Their diseases, and cure, 104.

Chaffinch, description and character, page 27. Cruel custom of blinding these birds condemned, 27. Marks of the cock and hen, 28. The time and manner of building their nest, 29. Of the young, and how to order them, 30. How to take them with nets, 30.

GOLDFINCH, description and character, 20. Its mild and gentle nature, and great docility in learning to draw up water, &c. 21. Fond of admiring itself in a looking-glass placed in their cage, 22. The age of this bird; marks of the cock and hen; 22. Time, manner, &c. of building their nest, 23. Of the young, how to order them, 23. Diseases, and cure, 25. Time and seasons for catching them, 25.

Green-

INDEX.

Green-bird, see Greenfinch.

Greenfinch, description and character, page 31. Marks of the cock and hen, 31. The time and manner of their building, 32. Of the young, how to order them, 33.

Green-linnet, see Greenfinch.

HEDGE-SPARROW, description and character, 89. Of their building, &c.; their young, and how to order them; 90.

LINNET, common one, description and character, 34. Marks of the cock and hen, 34. Time and manner of their building, 35. Of the young, how to order them, &c. 36. The diseases, and their cure, 37. How to catch and order these birds; 39.

NIGHTINGALE, description and character, page 73. Marks of the cock and hen, 74. Time and manner of building their nest, &c. 75. Of their nest, with directions for finding it, 75. Of the young, how to order them, 76. Their diseases, and cure, 77. The seasons, and various ways to take Branchers and old Nightingales, and to order them when taken, 80.

RED-BIRD, see Red Grosbeak.
Red Grosbeak, description and character, page 84.
Red-pole, description and character, page 66.
Red-start, description, character, and marks of the cock and hen, page 68. Of their breeding; when to take, and how to order their young, &c. 68. Of the strange dogged temper of this bird, 69.
Reed-sparrow, description, character, and colour of their eggs, 88.
Robin-red-breast, description and character; its manner of feeding when wild; page 61. Marks of the cock and hen; time and manner of building their nest; 62. Colour of her eggs; of the young, how to order them; 63.

SKY-LARK, description and character, page 41. To know the cock from the hen, 42. Time and manner of building their nest, &c 43. Of the young, how to order them, &c. 43. Their diseases, and cures; several ways of catching them; to take Pushers; 46. To take Branchers, 47.

Starling,

INDEX.

Starling, description and character; marks of the cock and hen; page 12. Time and manner of building her nest, 13. Of the young, how to order them; the method of slitting their tongues, to make them talk plainer, is a cruel and useless expedient, 14. Diseases and cures, 15.

THRUSH, description and character; different kinds of Thrushes; their description and characters; page 6. Marks of the cock and hen, 7. The time and manner of building her nest, 8. Of their young, and how to order them, 10. Their natural food, 11.

Thistle-finch, see Goldfinch.

Tit-lark, description and character; marks of the cock and hen; page 59. Of their nest; method of catching, managing, feeding, and taming them; 60.

Twite, description and character, page 40.

VIRGINIA-Nightingale, see Red-Grosbeak.

WOOD-LARK, description and character, page 50. Marks of the cock and hen, 52. Time and manner of their building; of the young, how to order them; 53. The season for catching these birds, and how to order them when taken, 55.

Wren, description and character; marks of the cock and hen; page 70. Time and manner of their building; of the young, how to order them; 71.

YELLOW-hammer, description, character, method of building, &c. 86.

www.ingramcontent.com/pod-product-compliance
Lightning Source LLC
Chambersburg PA
CBHW030257170426
43202CB00009B/777